× **MAYBE** ×

Swearing

××

WILL HELP

××××××××××××

**RELAX AND CURSE YOUR ASS OFF
IN CROSS-STITCH**

× MAYBE ×

Swearing

××

WILL HELP

xxxxxxxxxxxx

RELAX AND CURSE YOUR ASS OFF
IN CROSS-STITCH

weldon**owen**

Contents

INTRODUCTION

We all need a release these days. The stress of just living is enough to need one, but then there's that jerk who cut you off in traffic, the seemingly never-ending stream of what-in-the-actual-fuck news . . . it's enough to make you lose your shit sometimes.

Believe it or not, cross-stitch is an actual proven stress-reliever (the people at the American Home Sewing Association actually did a study on it!). In a world filled with chaos, cross-stitching gives a sense of gaining control over something (choosing your own pattern, working at your own pace), and the soothing aspect of repetitive motion helps to lower blood pressure, decrease heart rate, and reduce stress. More than anything, an evening stabbing a piece of cloth with a needle can just make you fucking happy.

Which, of course, is all well and good, but for some of us, stitching "home sweet home" just isn't going to cut it. Sometimes, there is nothing more stress-relieving than letting loose with a good curse word. So we thought, fuck it (page 110), let's combine the two and really get our relaxation on!

We've gathered a group of some of today's best cross-stitch artists, all of whom have let their curse and snark flags fly. Their unique styles range from traditional samplers and florals to retro Eighties and tattoo art. There are pieces for every skill level, and every level of cursing, From wishing you were a unicorn so you could stab stupid people with your head (page 26), to telling that dumbshit to suck it (page 114). Each piece is a blast to stitch. For those who are less inclined to the harder stuff, you can curse like a Brit ("Bollocks," page 18), embrace your inner yogi with a good "Namaste bitches" (page 40), or just let go with a good "SHUT UP" (page 50).

But it's not just about the relaxation you get while stitching the pieces. Each pattern in this book was chosen for its stress-relieving sentiments. So, when things are getting a bit rough, you can look at that "Oh HELL No" (page 88) piece on your wall and let it be your calming touchstone.

We all need that release. We all need to relax and find calm in the chaos. And maybe stitching naughty words onto fabric will bring us all a little inner fucking peace.

Happy damn stitching!

THE BASICS

Cross-stitch is easy. Here's what you
need, and how to do it.

WHAT IN THE HELL DO I NEED?

Luckily, you don't have to break the bank to start cross-stitching. A hoop, some floss (thread), fabric, and a needle are all you need. You can get super fancy and buy all kinds of accessories, but don't feel like you have to—a pair of regular scissors will cut floss just as well as those gorgeous little embroidery scissors! So, let's talk about the basics:

The Fabric

Technically, cross-stitch can be done on any kind of fabric, but for this book we are only using Aida cloth. Aida is a cloth that is made specifically for cross-stitch, and it is woven in such a way that it looks like a grid with holes at even intervals, so you know exactly where your needle goes. Aida cloth comes in an array of colors, so don't think you always have to use white. Aida also comes in precut sizes as well as rolls that you can cut to size; if you're planning on doing more than one piece, your best bet is to buy the roll.

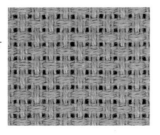

Aida cloth comes in different incounts in—the count refers to the number of holes per inch of fabric. The easiest to use is 14-count Aida (14 stitches to the inch). The higher the count, the tighter the stitches will be, and the smaller the final piece will be (and the more challenging it can be to stitch). Unless you need to fit a specific frame (or want a challenge!), we suggest sticking to 14-count Aida. In case you do want to play with the size, however, each pattern gives you the final piece size in different cloth counts.

The Floss

Cross-stitch is done with cotton embroidery floss, which is made up of six thin strands twisted together. There are several brands, but for this book we are using DMC®, which is one of the most common and accessible brands. For most of the patterns in this book you will use two strands, but in general, the cloth count determines how many of the six strands you will use:

11-count: 3 strands
12-count: 2-3 strands
14-count: 2-3 strands
16-count: 2 strands
18-count: 1-2 strands
20-count: 1 strand

MAKE IT BOLD

If you prefer a denser look to your finished work (so that the Xs look more like full blocks of color), use three strands of floss on 14-count. Don't go any higher, though—your piece will start to look clunky and stitching will be difficult. Remember, if you do go up to three strands, you will have to increase the amount of floss needed for the project.

The Needle

Since Aida cloth already has the holes in it, a tapestry needle is best to use, as it has a blunt tip. Tapestry needles come in a variety of sizes, and you want to make sure you don't use too large of a size—it will stretch the holes in your cloth and distort your project. For 14-count Aida, we recommend using a size 24 tapestry needle.

The Hoop

You always want to work your cross-stitch on a hoop; this keeps the fabric tight and your stitches neat and uniform. People have their preferences when it comes to the size of hoop to use; some prefer to work the pattern in sections, using smaller hoops that are easier to hold in your hand; others prefer to be able to have the entire pattern visible in the hoop. The choice is yours. There are also several kinds of frames—plastic, wood, screw frame, snap frame—but the most common and easiest to find are plastic and wood. Plastic tends to hold the fabric better, but the wood frame can transition easily from working hoop to display hoop.

A WORD ABOUT SCISSORS

As we said at the beginning, you don't need a special pair of scissors for cross-stitch—really, any scissors will do. However, a small pair of embroidery scissors does have one distinct advantage—their small, sharp points come in handy if you screw up and need to pull out stitches.

THE SETUP

Before we dive into stitching, let's get our cloth and thread ready.

Cutting the Cloth

Let's face it, mistakes happen in cross-stitch—miscounting stitches, running out of thread—and all of them can be fixed, except one: running out of fabric. There is no coming back from cutting your fabric too small and running out of room for the pattern! It's always best to leave yourself a healthy border of at least 3–4 in (7.5–10 cm) on each side. So, if your finished piece is 4 x 6 in (10 x 12 cm), your piece of fabric should be at least 10 x 12 in (25 x 30 cm). This may seem like a lot, but it's better to have excess than to run out! (It will also help when it comes time to mount your piece.) Each pattern in this book gives you the size cloth you need, including a healthy border.

Where in the Hell Do I Start?

It's always best to start stitching in the middle of the pattern; if you start in a corner and misjudge the placement, you could run out of fabric!

Finding the middle of your piece of cloth is easy: Just fold it in half lengthwise, then in half widthwise and press the folds with your finger. Open the fabric, and where the two creases intersect is your center. Insert your needle into this intersect so you won't lose your place when you pull the fabric taught in your hoop.

Getting It On (the Hoop)

Hoops have two parts—the inner (smaller) and outer (larger) hoop. On some hoops, the inner has a little lip that you can feel, which helps the fabric stay in place. If yours has that lip, that lip faces up. Place the outer hoop on a flat surface, then lay the fabric on top (that lip should now be against the fabric). Center the fabric, using the marked center as a guide. The outer hoop has a screw and nut at the top; unscrew it as far as you can without the nut falling off, then carefully place it on top of the fabric. Push it down until the two hoops meet and the fabric is taut. Tighten the screw just enough to hold the fabric, then pull the edges of the fabric to make it as tight as you want. (Some people like a little give, others like it as tight as a drum—it's up to you). One the fabric is taut, tighten the screw all the way.

Floss That Needle

Before threading the needle, we have to get the floss ready. Cut a piece of floss about the length of your forearm (from the tip of your finger to the crook of your arm). If you go any longer, you'll risk it tangling and knotting while you stitch, which is a bitch, to say the least. Take one end and hold it between your thumb and index finger. Rub the floss a little bit to separate the strands, then take two strands in one hand and the four in the other and slowly pull them apart. Set aside the four strands and thread your needle with the two. We're ready to go!

LET'S GET THIS SHOW ON THE ROAD!

Cross-stitch couldn't be simpler—it is just making a series of Xs, which are made up of two small stitches that cross diagonally. The Aida cloth makes it even simpler, by showing you exactly where your needle should go, so there is no guesswork! But before we get to the stitches, let's figure out how to read a pattern.

How to Read a Pattern

The patterns in this book are done in what is called counted cross-stitch. It is called that because you literally count the number of colored blocks on the pattern and stitch that number. To some, it may sound tedious, or intimidating, but it's actually much easier than working on a printed pattern, as sometimes the printing isn't done well or the pattern is printed crooked on the fabric, which it makes reading it a disaster. In counted cross-stitch, there is no guessing—if you have five red blocks, you make five red stitches. Easy peasy.

A cross-stitch pattern is made up of colored blocks on a grid (just like the grid of your cloth). Each block on the grid represents one X of cross-stitch. The colors correspond to the color chart, which tells you which color of floss to use. Some patterns that have several colors also include symbols in the colored blocks to make it even easier to determine which color you should use.

A couple of specifics on the patterns:

1. On each pattern you'll see two red lines—one vertical and one horizontal. These are to help you determine the center of your pattern—where they intersect is the center.

2. The grids have darker lines at every ten stitches, to help you with counting larger numbers of stitches.

BREAKING UP THE PATTERN

We have spread out the patterns over a couple of pages, in order to make the pattern larger and easier to use. To help navigate between pages, a repeat of five rows from the previous page is shown in gray—do not stitch the grayed-out section; it is only there for reference!

Where to Start

Don't listen to that singing nun—the very best place to start a cross-stitch project is in the middle, so that the pattern is centered on the canvas. But again, this is personal preference—if working from the center completely stresses you out, you can start from any point in the pattern. Count the number of stitches (blocks) from the center of the pattern (the intersection of the red lines) to the point you want to stitch, then count the same number of squares on your fabric, using the center you've marked as the reference.

To Knot or
Not to Knot

There are some cross-stitchers who will tell you never to knot your floss, and there are some reasons for not knotting. But what it really comes down to is this: how much you care about the back of your piece. Some people insist that the back has to look as pristine as the front, but, honestly, who is ever going to see the back? Don't let the back of your piece stress you out; if you're a beginner, or just don't give a rodent's hindquarters about the back (and why should you!), go ahead and knot your floss. Just simply tie a small knot in the end of your thread.

(One note: If you are planning to display your piece in a frame, it is best not to use knots, as they will leave lumps when mounted on the frame board. If you're displaying the piece in a hoop, you won't have to mount the piece on board, and knots will work just fine.)

If you want go no-knot, when you pull your thread through the first hole, hold about 1 in (2.5 cm) of thread on the back side with your finger. Keep holding it while you stitch the next few stitches over that thread. (This is called anchoring the thread.)

No matter if you use a knot or anchor, when you are finished with that thread, turn your piece over and work your needle under a couple of stitches, pull the thread through, and cut.

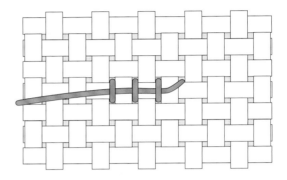

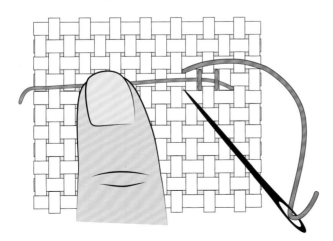

THE KNOTLESS LOOP

This is a neat and super-easy way to avoid a knot, if you're using two strands of floss. Cut a piece of floss twice the length you need, then only pull out a single strand instead of two. Bring the two ends of the single strand together, so you have a loop at the other end. Thread the side with the ends through the needle. Come up through the fabric for your first stitch, leaving the loop in back, then come back down and thread the needle through the loop. Gently pull until the loop flattens at the back.

THE STITCHES, BITCHES!

Okay, now that we're all ready with the fabric and needle, and we know how to read the pattern, it's time to learn how to do the damned stitch.

Single Cross-stitch

It couldn't be easier. A full stitch is made up of two diagonal stitches. Here's how you create one.

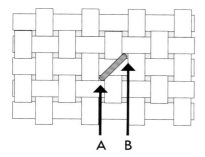

1. Make the first part of your X (/) by bringing your needle from the back through one hole (A). This will be the lower-left corner of your stitch. Pull your thread all the way through and insert your needle through the hole that is diagonally to the right (B) and pull the thread through. You should now have a diagonal stitch—the first part of your cross.

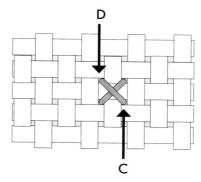

2. Now, bring your needle up through the lower-right corner hole (C), and then down through the upper-left corner hole (D).

That's it! You've made one complete stitch. Needless to say, if you ever have a pattern that includes a half stitch, you only make one of these diagonals.

Multiple Cross-stitches

If you have a number of the same color stitches to do, you can do all of the first diagonals together (/////) and then go back and do the second diagonals (\\\\\) together. To do this:

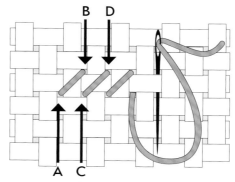

1. Come up through the bottom-left hole (A), go down into the top-right hole (B), come up again in the bottom-right hole (C), which is now the beginning of your next diagonal stitch, and the down into the next top-right hole (D). Repeat for as many full stitches as you need.

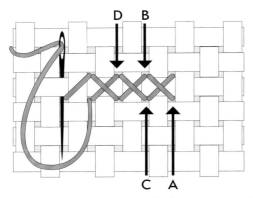

2. When you get to the end of your row, work back across the row to complete the stitches in the other direction.

This technique is also really handy when it comes to large sections of color—and can save lots of miscounting headaches. Stitch just the outline of a large color section with the first diagonal, then go back and fill in. This way, if you do miscount the outline, you're only pulling out a handful of single stitches!

Specialty Stitch: the Backstitch

Technically an embroidery stitch, the backstitch gives you a nice, unbroken line, which can look pretty against all of those Xs! (See the "Welcome to the Shitshow" pattern on page 94). It's just as easy as the cross-stitch:

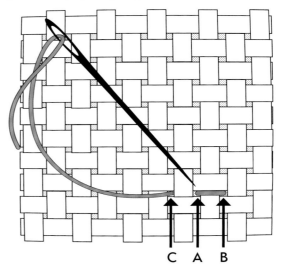

1. Bring your needle up from back to front (A). Take your needle down into hole to the horizontal right (this is B). This is one stitch.

2. For your second stitch, come up in the hole to the left of A (this is C), then back down into the hole of A. This is the back part of backstitch.

3. To make the next stitch, come up in the hole to the left of C, then down into C; continue to come up through the hole to the left in the line, and coming down into the hole of the previous stitch. You should now have a straight line!

Carrying the Thread

You've got little bits of green all over the pattern—do you have to cut the thread and restart for every section?

Not necessarily. If the sections are in close proximity, you can do what is called "carrying the thread" (which just means not cutting the thread between the sections). You only want to do this over two or three blank squares, at most—any more, and that carried thread can start showing through the holes in the fabric. If you're carrying across an area that's already stitched, you can go a little farther, but just weave your needle under the stitched section, to tack down that carried thread.

G★D F★CKING D@#MIT!

Fixing a Miscount

Miscounting stitches happens to everyone, no matter how experienced you are. It's just a fact of cross-stitch life! There is nothing worse than getting halfway through a pattern and realizing that two sections aren't matching up. The best advice is (to paraphrase the old carpenter's saying): count twice, stitch once. Stop occasionally and just do a quick check to make sure everything is lining up on the fabric as it is in the pattern. Better to find out sooner rather than later!

Don't stress if you've miscounted; the mistake is easily fixable. Just take your needle and pick out the wayward stitches. If it's a section that's already been completed, use a seam ripper or the tip of your embroidery scissors to clip out a few stitches (always working from the back), and then pick out the rest with your needle.

But, most importantly, don't beat yourself up or get stressed. It's all part of the process!

Out, Out, Damned Spot!

No matter how careful you are, your project may get soiled. No worries here, though—you can wash your piece! Just place it in a bowl of tepid water mixed with a mild laundry detergent, swish it around (don't rub or twist the fabric), and let it set. Then rinse (don't wring it out), lay it flat on a bath towel, and roll up the towel to squeeze out the excess water. Lay flat to dry.

Washing your piece is also great for getting out the circles that your hoop leaves in the cloth!

I'm Done Stabbing. Now What Do I Do?

Now that you've stabbed away all your aggression, it's time to show off your piece. There are lots of ways you can do it, all of which are pretty easy. But first, you have to get the piece ready for framing.

Prepping Your Piece

Before you frame, you might want to wash your fabric (see above). Not only will this get the fabric clean, but it will also remove the indents left by the hoop. Whether you wash the fabric or not, you're definitely going to need to iron it. Put a clean, white dish towel down on your ironing board. Lay the piece face-down and place another dish towel on top. With your iron set on steam, slowly press the piece until the creases are gone.

Hooping Your Piece

For this, you'll need a nice bamboo or wood hoop and some all-purpose glue. Place your piece in the hoop, making sure the piece is centered and it is nice and taut. Make sure the screw closure is centered as well, because that is what you are going to use to hang it. Trim the leftover fabric down to about 1 in (2.5 cm)—you want just enough to fold inside that bottom hoop. Draw a thin line of glue around the inside of the bottom hoop, then press your leftover fabric border into the glue line.

Framing Your Piece

There are a lot of ways you can go here—from professional framing to just taping your piece to a board and putting it in a frame. If you're using a photo frame, the easiest way is to trim your piece, leaving about one inch of border, place it in the frame, then insert the back of the frame so the border hangs over the side, then tack down the border to the back of the frame (or don't—it's the back of the piece, so who's going to see it?).

If you're worried about wrinkles, a great alternative is to use self-adhesive mounting board. This board has one side with a strong adhesive; just cut it to the size you need (if you're putting it in a frame, use the back of the frame as your guide), peel off the sticky side, and place your piece on it (you can lift it up and rearrange as much as you like). Press down to smooth out any wrinkles, then place it in the frame.

THE ONLY CROSS-STITCH RULE: DO IT YOUR WAY

The beauty of cross-stitch is that there really isn't a wrong way to do it—no wrong way to hold your hoop, work a pattern, or even mount your piece. If you find a way of stitching that works better than how we have described it here, go for it! If you want to knot your floss or use a frame rather than a hoop, why not? A friend got so stressed out about the back of her piece not being perfect because her mom said that was "the rule" that she couldn't even get started. But there are no rules. Do what works for you. Once you start stitching, you'll find your own pace and your own style—and the inner peace that can come from stabbing something lots and lots of times.

HAVE FUN!

THE PATTERNS

BOLLOCKS

Design by Stephanie Rohr of stephXstitch

When you want to curse like a proper Brit.

COLOR CHART

COLOR BLOCK	FLOSS NUMBER	COLOR NAME	STITCHES	STRANDS	SKEINS
▶	353	Peach	138	2	1
♥	471	Very Light Avocado Green	128	2	1
☾	807	Peacock Blue	243	2	1
▣	815	Medium Garnet	102	2	1
↗	820	Very Dark Royal Blue	112	2	1
♠	3855	Light Autumn Gold	78	2	1

ICYDK

Bollocks is British slang for a part of a man's anatomy (look it up). Much like *fuck*, it's used a hundred different ways—from a straight-up expletive expressing frustration ("Oh, BOLLOCKS!") to describing a particularly loathsome person ("Who's that old bollocks bothering the waitress?") to screwing something up ("Boy, Gary sure did bollocks that interview!") or just calling someone out on their bullshit ("That's a load of bollocks!"). You can't go wrong tossing around *bollocks*.

PATTERN INFORMATION

FABRIC: 14-count Aida, 12 x 11 in (30.5 x 28 cm)

NEEDLE: Size 24 tapestry

STITCH COUNT: 51 x 43

FINISHED SIZE: 5.87 x 5 in (14.92 x 12.7 cm)

MOUNTING: 6 or 7 in round hoop

SIZE VARIATIONS

12-count Aida: 4.25 x 3.58 in (10.8 x 9.09 cm)

16-count Aida: 3.19 x 2.69 in (8.1 x 6.83 cm)

18-count Aida: 2.83 x 2.39 in (7.19 x 6.07 cm)

Project shown is stitched on 14-count, white Aida cloth and mounted in a 6 in wood hoop.

COLOR CHART

COLOR BLOCK	FLOSS NUMBER
▶	353
♥	471
☽	807
■	815
⚑	820
♠	3855

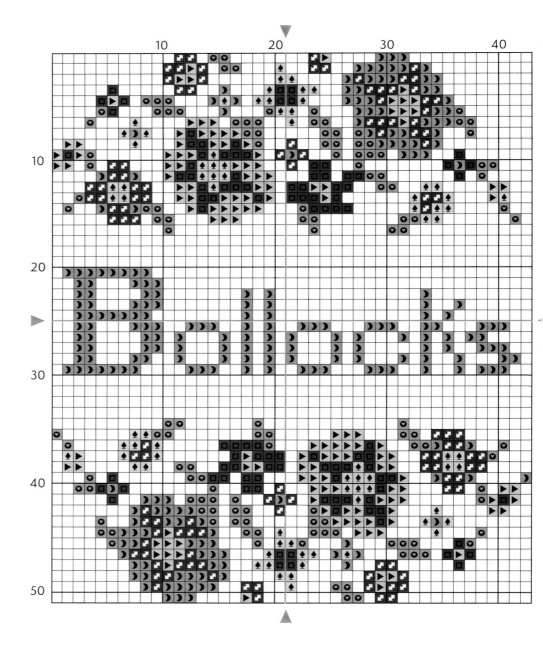

Stitch Your Own: Lowercase Alphabet

Throughout the book, we'll give you alphabets that you can use to modify any projects shown, or to make your own! You can even combine them to make something truly unique. If you want to make a bolder statement, see the Uppercase Alphabet on page 81. Have fun!

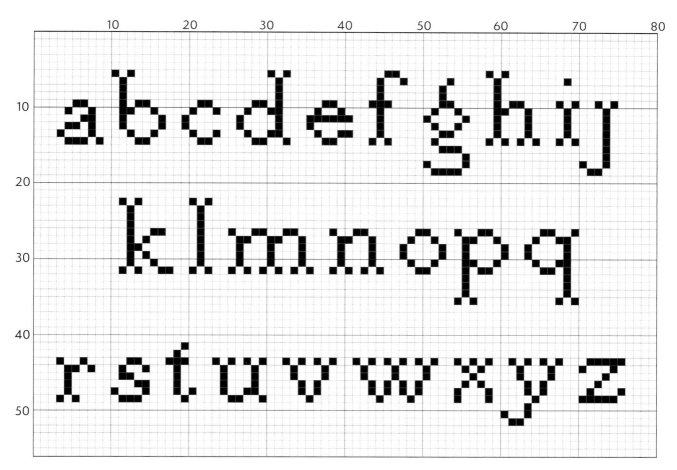

No Shit

Design by TheChillNeedle

The perfect retort for all of those Sherlocks out there.

COLOR CHART

COLOR BLOCK	FLOSS NUMBER	COLOR NAME	STITCHES	STRANDS	SKEINS
▌	666	Bright Red	1722	2	1
⫶	824	Very Dark Blue	2457	2	1
◗	964	Light Seagreen	2177	2	1

PATTERN INFORMATION

FABRIC: 14-count Aida, 17 x 12 in (43.2 x 30.5 cm)

NEEDLE: Size 24 tapestry

STITCH COUNT: 152 x 86

FINISHED SIZE: 10.9 x 6.1 in (27.6 x 15.6 cm)

MOUNTING: Piece will fit into 9 x 12 in picture frame or 12 in hoop

SIZE VARIATIONS

12-count Aida: 12.67 x 7.17 in (32.18 x 18.21 cm)

16-count Aida: 9.5 x 5.38 in (24.13 x 13.67 cm)

18-count Aida: 8.44 x 4.78 in (21.44 x 12.14 cm)

Project shown is stitched on 14-count, black Aida cloth and mounted in a 12 in wood hoop.

A LITTLE FUCKING HELP, PLEASE!

• Working with black Aida cloth can be tricky—it's hard to see the holes. Putting a white cloth or paper under the piece (on your lap, if that's how you're working) can make seeing the holes a little easier.

• The best way to work this pattern is first to stitch the outline of a block of color (say, a letter) with a single diagonal stitch (the first part of your cross), then go back and fill it in. This way, if you miscount, you only have to rip out a handful of half stitches in the outline, rather than realizing a mistake too late and having to rip out an entire stitched section!

COLOR CHART

COLOR BLOCK	FLOSS NUMBER
I	666
:	824
ϲ	964

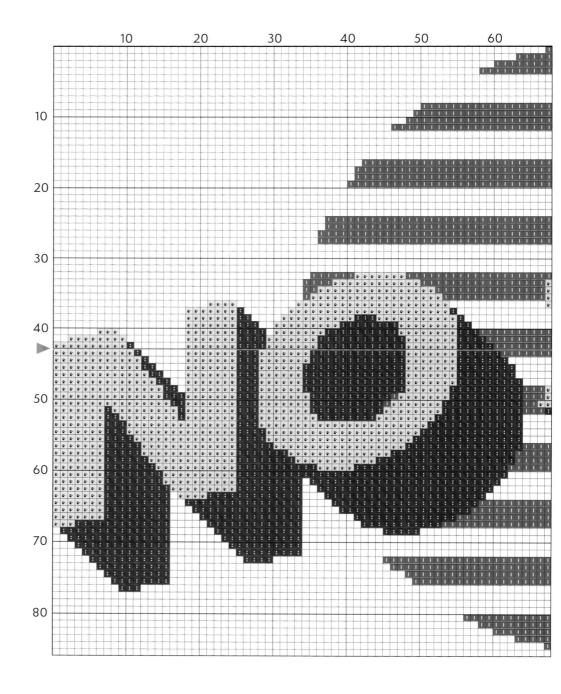

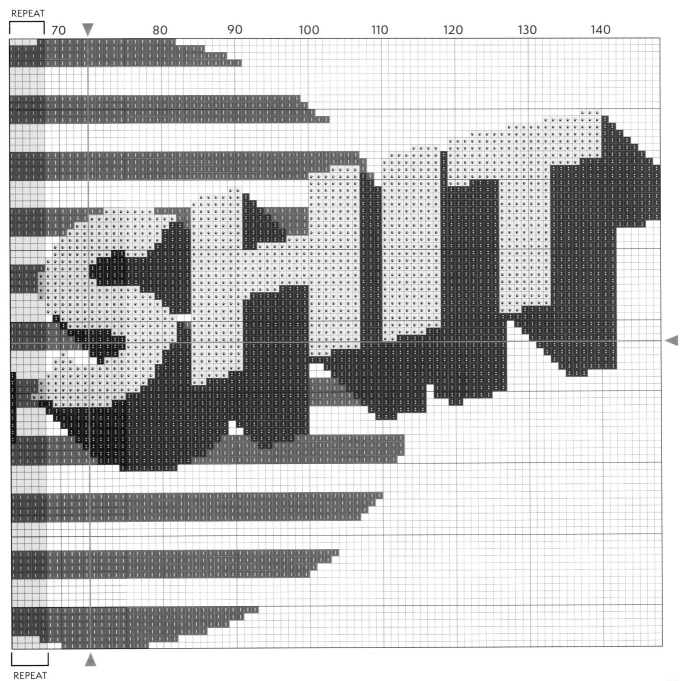

I wish I was
a Unicorn so
I could stab
stupid people
with my head

I Wish I Was A Unicorn So I Could Stab Stupid People With My Head

XXXXXXXXXXXXXXXXXXXXXXXXXXXXXXXX

Design by Aliton Embroidery

The added benefit of being a unicorn.

COLOR CHART

COLOR BLOCK	FLOSS NUMBER	COLOR NAME	STITCHES	STRANDS	SKEINS
L	666	Bright Red	200	2	1
a	699	Green	436	2	1
m	701	Light Green	918	2	1
x	726	Light Topaz	134	2	1
H	3705	Dark Melon	1277	2	1

PATTERN INFORMATION

FABRIC: 14-count Aida, 12 x 12 in (30.5 x 30.5 cm)

NEEDLE: Size 24 tapestry

STITCH COUNT: 127 x 107

FINISHED SIZE: 9 x 7.6 in (22.9 x 19.3 cm)

MOUNTING: Piece will fit into a 10 in hoop

SIZE VARIATIONS

12-count Aida: 10.58 x 8.92 in (26.87 x 22.66 cm)

14-count Aida: 9.07 x 7.64 in (23.04 x 19.41 cm)

18-count Aida: 7.06 x 5.94 in (17.93 x 15.09 cm)

Project shown is stitched on 14-count, ivory Aida cloth and mounted in a 10 in hoop.

COLOR CHART

COLOR BLOCK	FLOSS NUMBER
L	666
a	699
m	701
x	726
H	3705

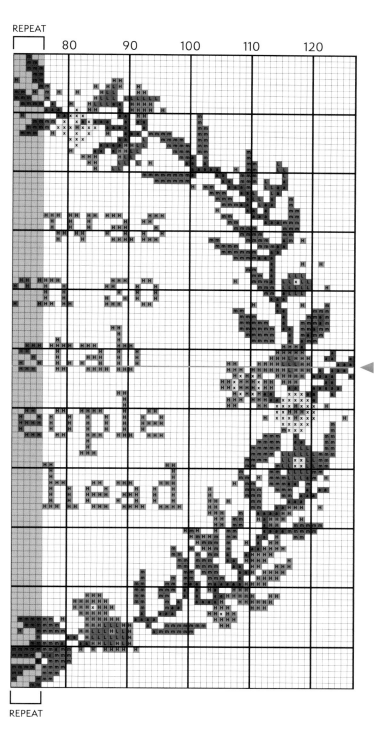

WASH YOUR DAMN HANDS

Design by Stitchy Little Fox

A little snark for the bathroom.

COLOR CHART

COLOR BLOCK	FLOSS NUMBER	COLOR NAME	STITCHES	STRANDS	SKEINS
◇◇	209	Dark Lavender	128	2	1
■	310	Black	412	2	1
4	327	Dark Violet	248	2	1
••	740	Tangerine	44	2	1
9	743	Medium Yellow	84	2	1
>	891	Dark Carnation	172	2	1
▼	894	Very Light Carnation	72	2	1
#	909	Very Dark Emerald Green	320	2	1
:	911	Medium Emerald Green	164	2	1
·|·	973	Bright Canary	50	2	1
1	3843	Electric Blue	230	2	1
/	3845	Medium Bright Turquoise	74	2	1

PATTERN INFORMATION

FABRIC: 14-count Aida, 12 x 12 in (30.5 x 30.5 cm)

NEEDLE: Size 24 tapestry

STITCH COUNT: 83 x 70

FINISHED SIZE: 5.75 x 5 in (14.92 x 12.7 cm)

MOUNTING: Piece will fit into an 8 x 10 in frame

SIZE VARIATIONS

12-count Aida: 6.92 x 5.83 in (17.58 x 14.81 cm)

14-count Aida: 5.93 x 5 in (15.06 x 12.7 cm)

18-count Aida: 4.61 x 3.89 in (11.71 x 9.88 cm)

Project shown is stitched on 14-count, white Aida cloth and mounted in a 7.5 x 9.5 in frame.

COLOR CHART

COLOR BLOCK	FLOSS NUMBER
◇◇	209
■	310
4	327
••	740
9	743
>	891
▼	894
#	909
:	911
·|·	973
1	3843
/	3845

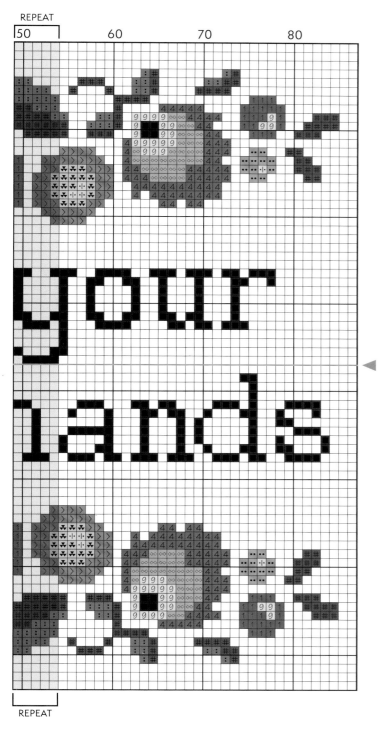

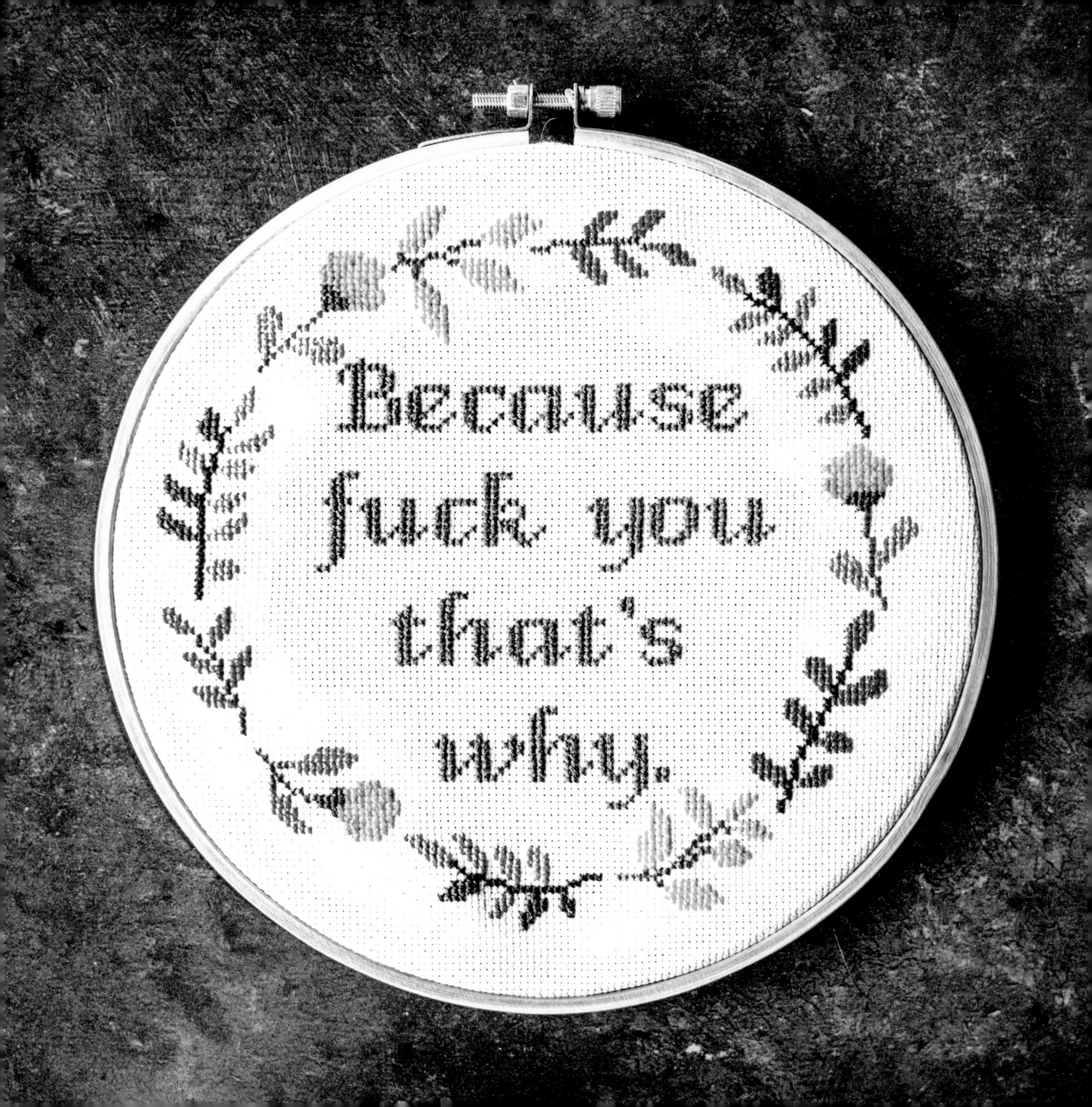
Because
fuck you
that's
why.

Because Fuck You That's Why.

Design by Oh Wow Stitch

When you really need them to stop it with all the questions.

COLOR CHART

COLOR BLOCK	FLOSS NUMBER	COLOR NAME	STITCHES	STRANDS	SKEINS
♡	379	Very Dark Pewter Gray	708	2	1
⊃	502	Blue Green	106	2	1
✖	610	Dark Drab Brown	139	2	1
△	646	Dark Beaver Gray	114	2	1
◎	742	Light Tangerine	97	2	1
▽	898	Very Dark Coffee Brown	96	2	1
◀	964	Light Seagreen	250	2	1
★	993	Very Light Aquamarine	47	2	1
◖	3782	Light Mocha Brown	235	2	1
◜	3817	Light Celadon Green	94	2	1
☽	3849	Light Teal Green	115	2	1
▢	3852	Very Dark Straw	81	2	1

PATTERN INFORMATION

FABRIC: 14-count Aida, 12 x 12 in (30.5 x 30.5 cm)

NEEDLE: Size 24 tapestry

STITCH COUNT: 110 x 109

FINISHED SIZE: 7.85 x 7.85 in (19.9 x 19.9 cm)

MOUNTING: Piece will fit into an 8 x 10 in frame

SIZE VARIATIONS

12-count Aida: 9.17 x 9.08 in (23.29 x 23.06 cm)

14-count Aida: 7.86 x 7.79 in (19.96 x 19.79 cm)

18-count Aida: 6.11 x 6.06 in (15.52 x 15.39 cm)

Project shown is stitched on 14-count, white Aida cloth and mounted in an 8 in hoop.

STITCHING NOTE

For a denser-looking stitch, Oh Wow Stitch suggests working the pattern on 16-count Aida; however, if you prefer a more "cross-stitch" look, where the Xs are more visible (as shown in the photo here), use 14-count Aida.

COLOR CHART

COLOR BLOCK	FLOSS NUMBER
♡	379
🖵	502
✖	610
⟁	646
○	742
▽	898
◀	964
★	993
◗	3782
◖	3817
☽	3849
◰	3852

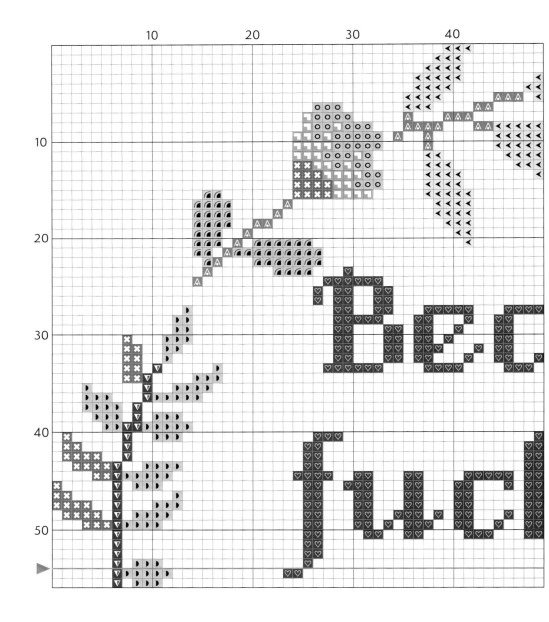

COLOR CHART

COLOR BLOCK	FLOSS NUMBER
♡	379
⊃	502
✖	610
◭	646
○	742
▽	898
◀	964
★	993
◗	3782
◖	3817
☽	3849
◻	3852

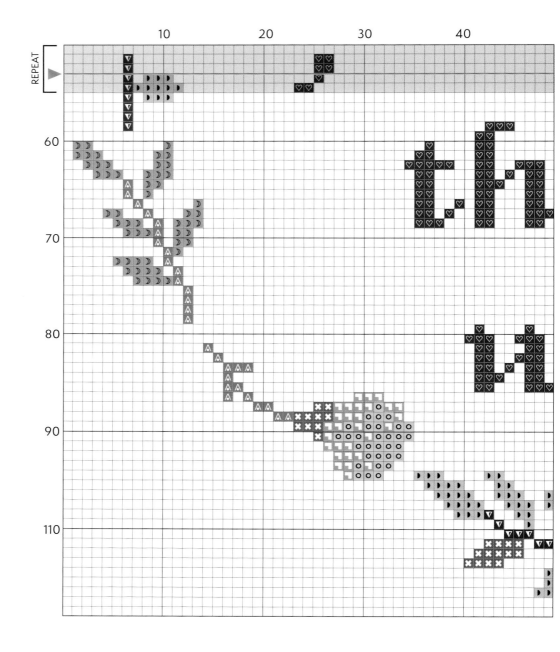

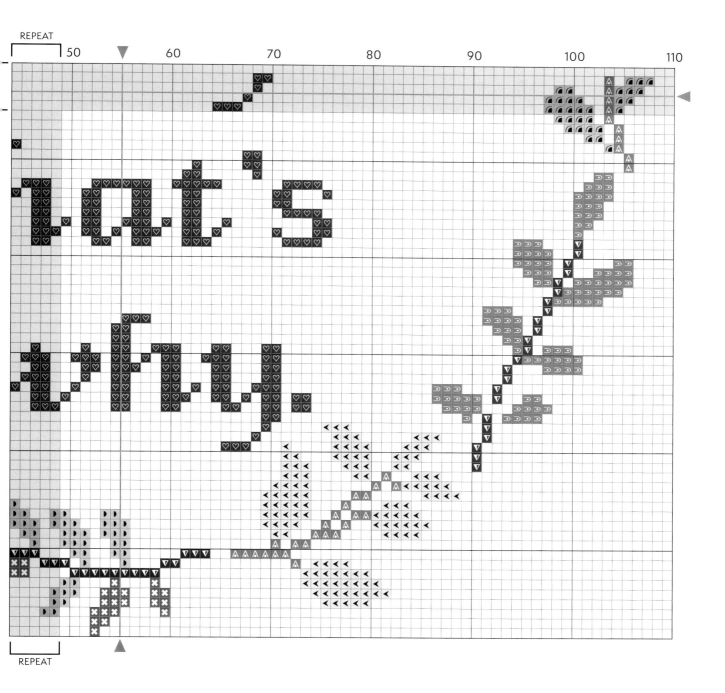

NAMASTE

bitches

NAMASTE BITCHES

XXXXXXXXXXXXXXXXXXXXXXXXXXXXXXXXXX

Design by Stitchy Little Fox

When you need to get Zen with your sarcasm.

COLOR CHART

COLOR BLOCK	FLOSS NUMBER	COLOR NAME	STITCHES	STRANDS	SKEINS
◖	742	Light Tangerine	29	2	1
4	744	Pale Yellow	21	2	1
▣	921	Copper	1	2	1
●	3345	Dark Hunter Green	2	2	1
8	3347	Medium Yellow Green	8	2	1
♥	3348	Light Yellow Green	38	2	1
△	3823	Ultra Pale Yellow	27	2	1
━●	310	Black	13 in (backstitch/french knot)	2	1
━	921	Copper	7 in (backstitch)	2	1
━	3345	Dark Hunter Green	10 in (backstitch)	2	1

PATTERN INFORMATION

FABRIC: 14-count Aida, 12 x 10 in (30.5 x 25.4 cm)

NEEDLE: Size 24 tapestry

STITCH COUNT: 34 x 22

FINISHED SIZE: 2.4 x 1.5 in (5.08 x 2.54 cm)

MOUNTING: Piece will fit into a 5 x 7 in picture frame

SIZE VARIATIONS

12-count Aida: 2.83 x 1.83 in (7.19 x 4.65 cm)

16-count Aida: 2.13 x 1.38 in (5.41 x 3.51 cm)

18-count Aida: 1.89 x 1.22 in (4.8 x 3.1 cm)

Project shown is stitched on 14-count, white Aida cloth and mounted in a 5 in hoop.

SPECIAL SYMBOLS

- • French knot (see page 43)
- — Backstitch (see page 14)

COLOR CHART

COLOR BLOCK	FLOSS NUMBER
⬤ (⊖)	742
4	744
▣	921
⬤	3345
8	3347
♥	3348
△	3823
━━●	310
━━	921
━━	3345

SPECIAL SYMBOLS

- • French knot (see page 43)
- — Backstitch (see page 14)

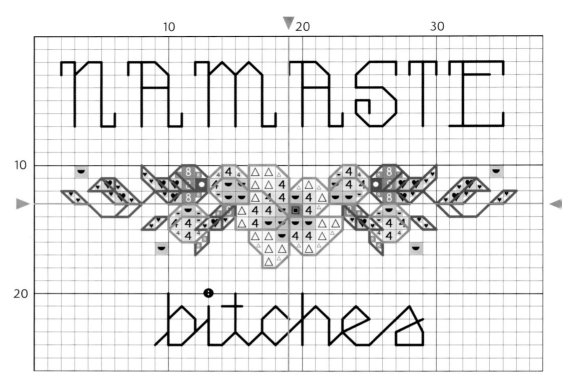

A LITTLE FUCKING HELP, PLEASE!

To make the stitches easier to see, here is the pattern without the backstitch. Do the cross-stitching first, then the backstitching. The tiny stitches are **quarter stitches**. To make them, come up through the hole that is closest to where the stitch is positioned in the square. Then, instead of going back down into a premade hole, take your needle through the middle of the square.

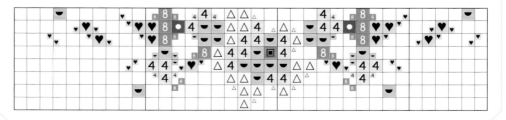

How to Make a French Knot

The "I" in *bitches* is dotted with a French Knot. Here's how you make it.

1. On the back of your project, secure your thread by running it under several stitches (you can knot it, but if you are mounting your piece in a frame, that knot could create a bump under your project).

2. Come up in the hole above the "I." This is A on the diagram.

3. Now, rest your hoop on your lap or on the table. You're going to need both hands on top of the project for this next part.

4. With one hand, hold the thread taut, about an inch or so away from the fabric. With your other hand, bring your needle right next to the thread, and wind the thread around the needle twice, from front to back. Gently pull the thread to keep it taut.

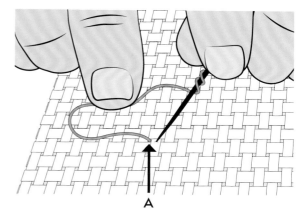

5. Keeping that thread taut, push the tip of your needle into the fabric right next to point A—you are not going in the next hole, but right into the fabric; this will help anchor the knot (don't pull it all the way through yet). Again, keeping the thread taut, pull the loops on the needle down so that they are resting on the fabric.

6. Take your needle hand under the hoop and gently push the needle and thread through. Keep holding that thread on top taut with the other hand until the needle is all the way through, then use your thumbnail to hold the thread down until it is completely pulled through.

The High
Road Sucks
as I am Petty
and Vindictive
by Nature

THE HIGH ROAD SUCKS AS I AM PETTY AND VINDICTIVE BY NATURE

xxxxxxxxxxxxxxxxxxxxxxxxxxxxxxxxxx

Design by Snarky Stitch Bitch

Just giving fair warning.

COLOR CHART

COLOR BLOCK	FLOSS NUMBER	COLOR NAME	STITCHES	STRANDS	SKEINS
◆	13	Medium Light Nile Green	139	2	1
▶	18	Yellow Plum	14	2	1
✳	20	Shrimp	415	2	1
⊙	156	Medium Light Blue Violet	44	2	1
⠿	166	Medium Light Moss Green	59	2	1
⬠	221	Very Dark Shell Pink	272	2	1
Z	315	Medium Dark Antique Mauve	45	2	1
〰	350	Medium Coral	18	2	1
◤	351	Coral	71	2	1
◀	352	Light Coral	85	2	1
≫	413	Dark Pewter Gray	768	2	1
✂	563	Light Jade	199	2	1
◗	645	Very Dark Beaver Gray	243	2	1
◂▸	761	Light Salmon	42	2	1
⏃	830	Dark Golden Olive	30	2	1
⬍	832	Golden Olive	133	2	1
◎	963	Ultra Very Light Dusty Rose	66	2	1
·‖·	967	Very Light Apricot	156	2	1
▨	3713	Very Light Salmon	15	2	1
◥	3847	Dark Teal Green	117	2	1
⠿	3849	Light Teal Green	15	2	1

PATTERN INFORMATION

FABRIC: 14-count Aida, 14 x 14 in (35.6 x 35.6 cm)

NEEDLE: Size 24 tapestry

STITCH COUNT: 111 x 108

FINISHED SIZE: 7.9 x 7.6 in (20 x 19.3 cm)

MOUNTING: Piece will fit into an 8 or 9 in embroidery hoop or a 9 in square picture frame

SIZE VARIATIONS

12-count Aida: 9.25 x 9 in (23.5 x 22.86 cm)

16-count Aida: 6.94 x 6.75 in (17.63 x 17.15 cm)

18-count Aida: 6.17 x 6 in (15.67 x 15.24 cm)

Project shown in stitched on 14-count, ivory Aida cloth, and mounted in an 8 in hoop.

COLOR CHART

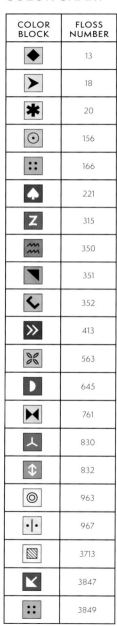

COLOR BLOCK	FLOSS NUMBER
◆	13
▶	18
✳	20
⊙	156
⁛	166
♠	221
Z	315
∿	350
◣	351
◄	352
≫	413
✶	563
D	645
⋈	761
⊥	830
⇕	832
◎	963
·|·	967
▨	3713
◥	3847
⁚⁚	3849

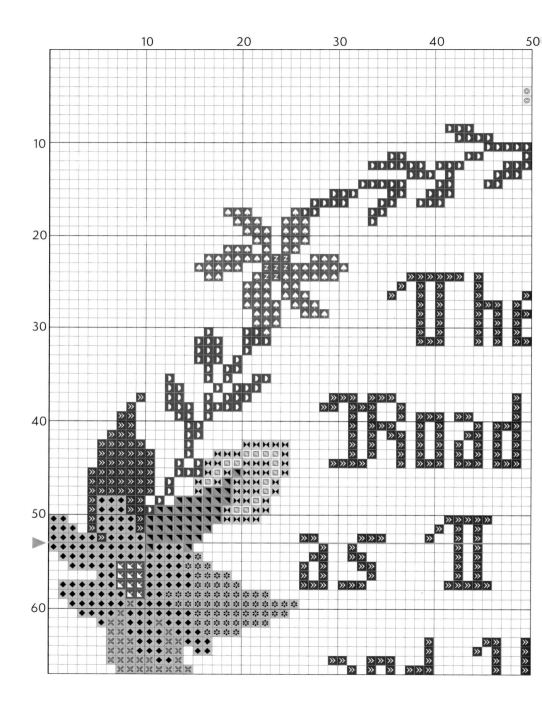

46

COLOR CHART

COLOR BLOCK	FLOSS NUMBER
◆	13
▶	18
✳	20
⊙	156
∷	166
♠	221
Z	315
∿	350
◣	351
◀	352
≫	413
✿	563
◗	645
◒	761
⅄	830
⇕	832
◎	963
•|•	967
▨	3713
◤	3847
∷	3849

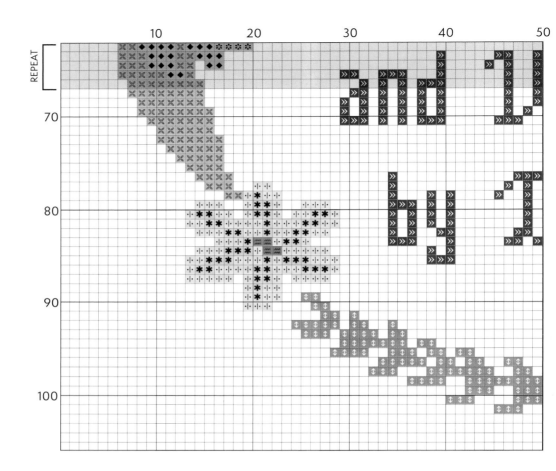

48

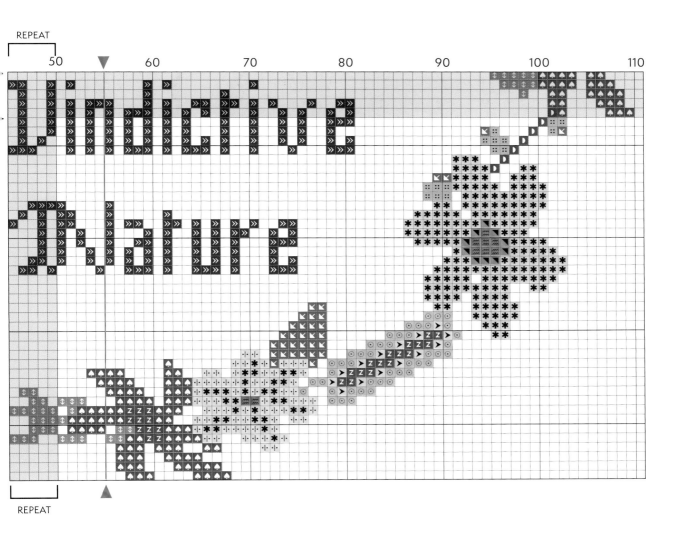

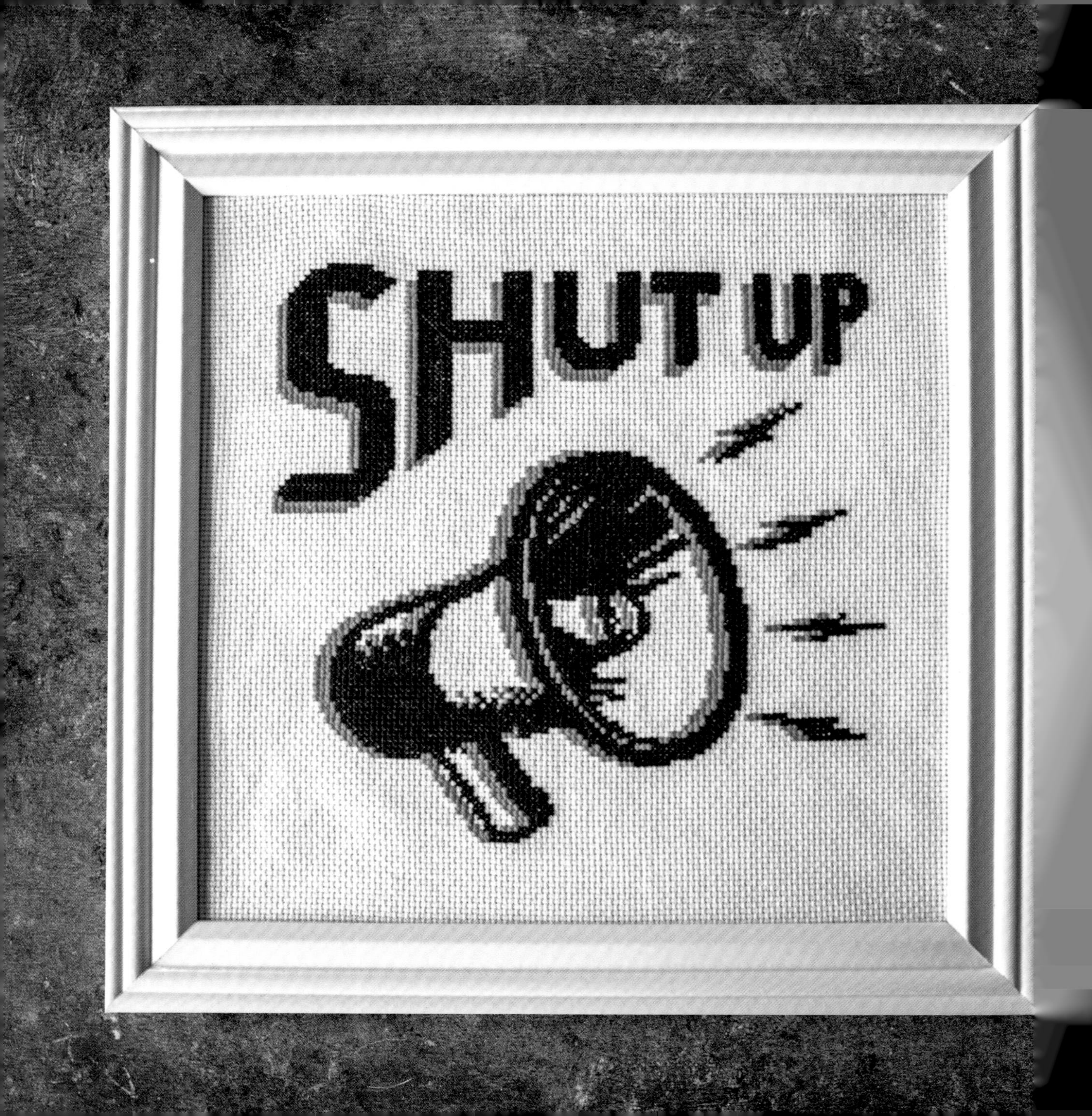
SHUT UP

Shut Up

Design by TheChillNeedle

Sometimes you just need a damned bullhorn.

COLOR CHART

COLOR BLOCK	FLOSS NUMBER	COLOR NAME	STITCHES	STRANDS	SKEINS
■	310	Black	3104	2	2
▨	946	Medium Burnt Orange	1219	2	1

PATTERN INFORMATION

FABRIC: 14-count Aida, 14 x 14 in (35.6 x 35.6 cm)

NEEDLE: Size 24 tapestry

STITCH COUNT: 114 x 112

FINISHED SIZE: 8 x 8 in (19.6 x 18.9 cm)

MOUNTING: Piece will fit into a 9 in or 10 in square picture frame

SIZE VARIATIONS

12-count Aida: 9 x 8.67 in (22.86 x 22.02 cm)

16-count Aida: 6.75 x 6.5 in (17.15 x 16.51 cm)

18-count Aida: 6 x 5.78 in (15.24 x 14.68 cm)

Project shown is stitched on 14-count, white Aida and mounted in a 10 x 10 in frame.

A LITTLE FUCKING HELP, PLEASE!

There is a lot of counting in this one, so here is a time-saving (and possibly headache-reducing) tip: Stitch the entire piece (or sections, if you like) in a single diagonal stitch (the first half of the cross-stitch); that way, if you miscount, you only have single stitches to rip out. Also, when you go back to fill in the other half of the stitches, you won't have to be tied to the book—the pattern is right in front of you!

COLOR CHART

COLOR BLOCK	FLOSS NUMBER
⬛	310
🟫	946

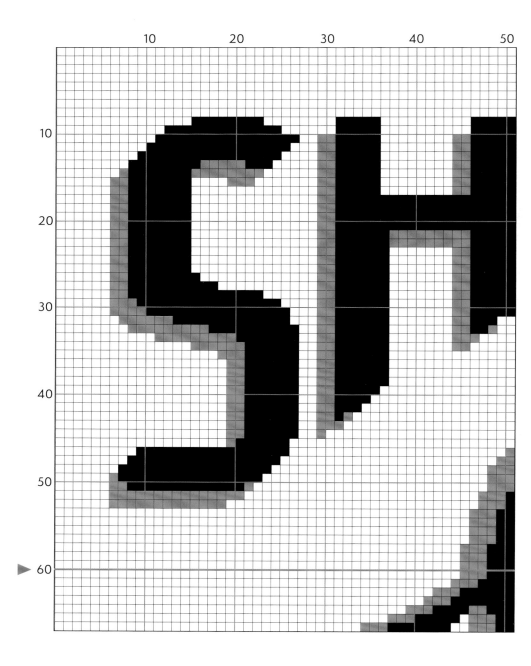

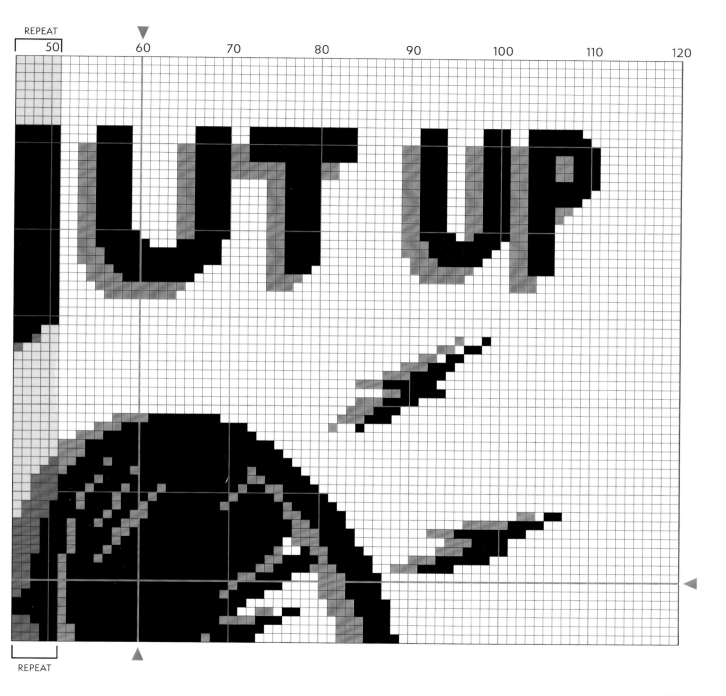

COLOR CHART

COLOR BLOCK	FLOSS NUMBER
⬛	310
🟫	946

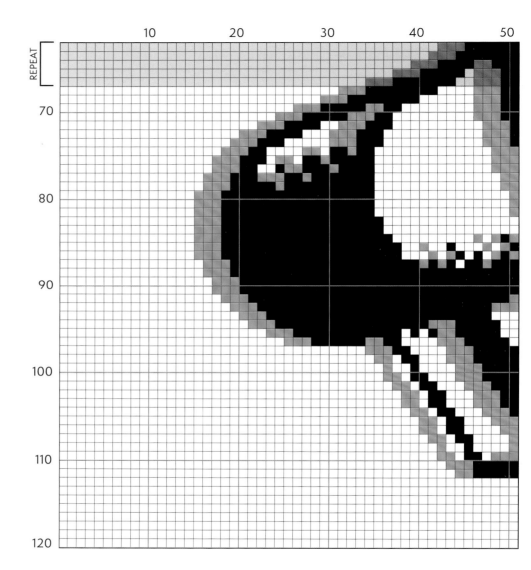

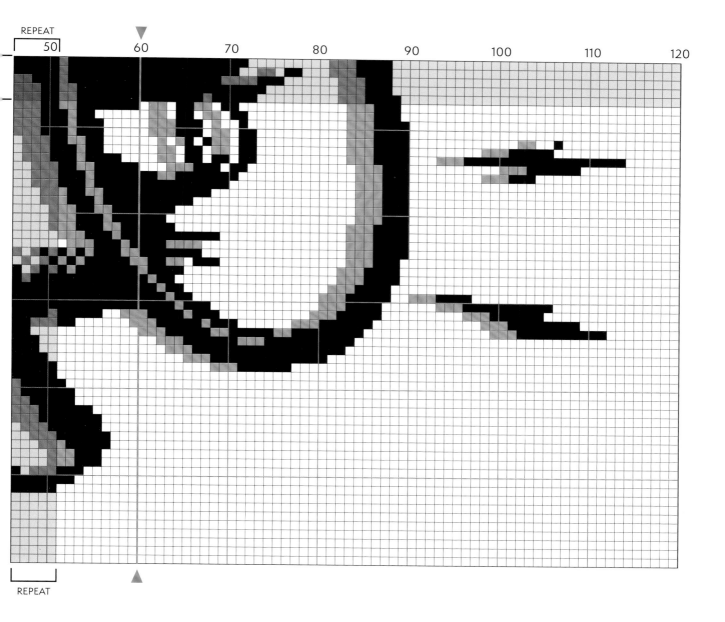

I'll Be Damned.

Design by 8 Bit Stitch

When you want to go old-school with your incredulity.

COLOR CHART

COLOR BLOCK	FLOSS NUMBER	COLOR NAME	STITCHES	STRANDS	SKEINS
■	310	Black	190	2	1
■	3346	Hunter Green	429	2	1
■	3687	Mauve	439	2	1

CUSTOMIZE YOUR SNARK

This phrase is a sentimental favorite of 8 Bit Stitch. To customize this with your own favorite word or phrase, use the alphabets on pages 21 and 81.

PATTERN INFORMATION

FABRIC: 14-count Aida, 12 x 10 in (30.5 x 25.4 cm)

NEEDLE: Size 24 tapestry

STITCH COUNT: 75 x 57

FINISHED SIZE: 5.4 x 4.1 in (13.6 x 10.3 cm)

MOUNTING: Piece will fit into a 5 x 7 in picture frame

SIZE VARIATIONS

12-count Aida: 6.25 x 4.75 in (15.86 x 12.07 cm)

16-count Aida: 4.69 x 3.56 in (11.91 x 9.04 cm)

18-count Aida: 4.17 x 3.17 in (10.59 x 8.05 cm)

Project shown is stitched on 14-count, white Aida cloth and is mounted in a 5 x 7 in frame.

COLOR CHART

COLOR BLOCK	FLOSS NUMBER
⬛	310
🟩	3346
🟪	3687

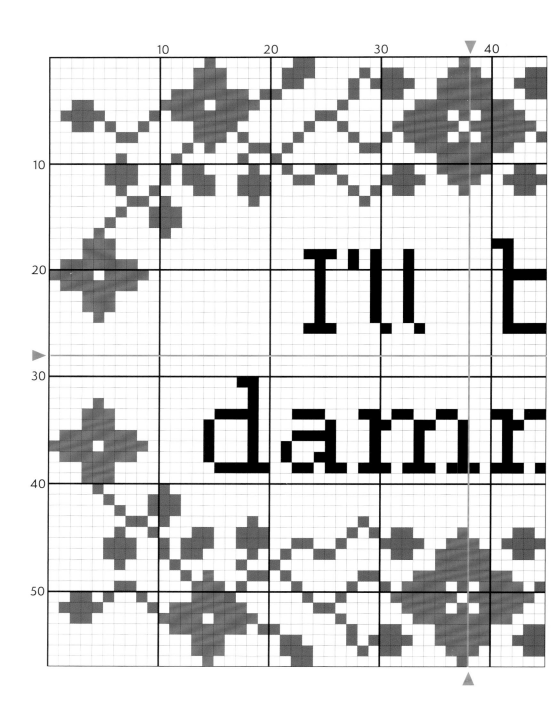

50   60   70

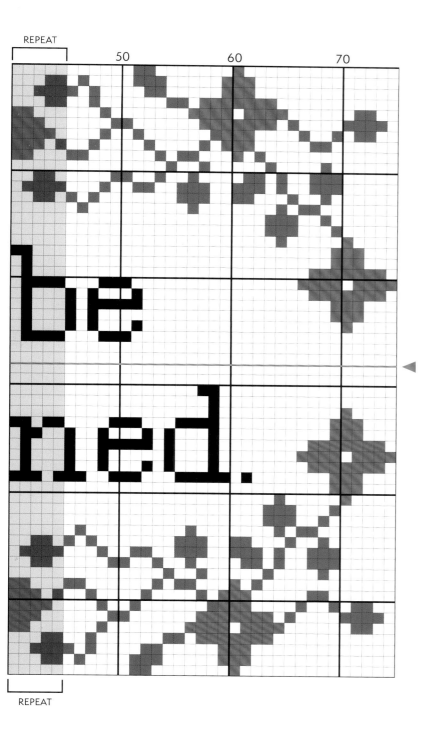

WHAT THE ACTUAL FUCK

XXXXXXXXXXXXXXXXXXXXXXXXXXXXX

Design by Happy Sloth

The snarky disbelief is high with this one.

COLOR CHART

COLOR BLOCK	FLOSS NUMBER	COLOR NAME	STITCHES	STRANDS	SKEINS
■	310	Black	2929	2	3

A LITTLE FUCKING HELP, PLEASE!

The best way to work this pattern is first to stitch the outline of the big blocks of color with a single diagonal stitch (the first part of your cross), then go back and fill it in. This way, if you miscount, you only have to rip out a handful of half stitches in the outline, rather than realizing a mistake too late and having to rip out an entire stitched section!

PATTERN INFORMATION

FABRIC: 14-count Aida, 15 x 13 in (38 x 33 cm)

NEEDLE: Size 24 tapestry

STITCH COUNT: 115 x 96

FINISHED SIZE: 8.2 x 6.9 in (21 x 17.5 cm)

MOUNTING: Piece will fit into an 8 x 10 in picture frame

SIZE VARIATIONS

12-count Aida: 9.58 x 8 in (24.56 x 20.32 cm)

14-count Aida: 8.21 x 6.86 in (20.85 x 17.42 cm)

18-count Aida: 6.39 x 5.33 in (16.23 x 13.53 cm)

Project shown is stitched on 14-count, white Aida cloth and is mounted in an 8 x 10 in frame.

COLOR CHART

COLOR BLOCK	FLOSS NUMBER
■	310

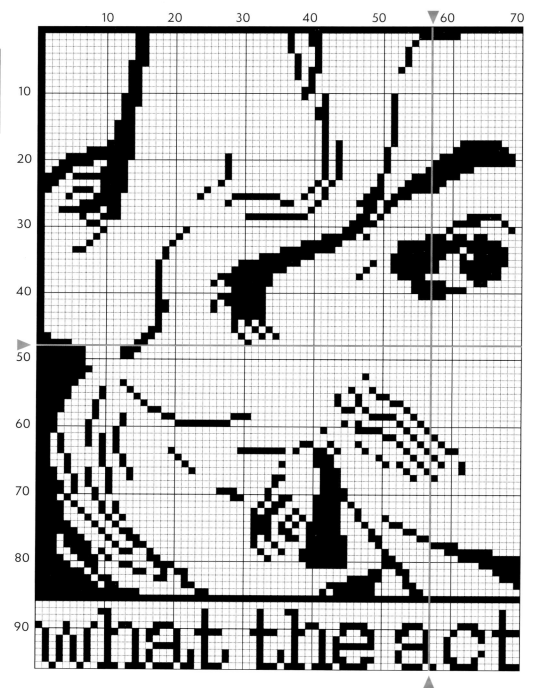

80   90   100   110

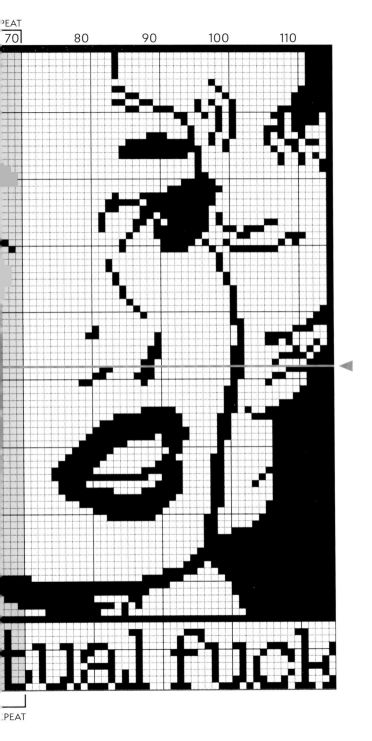

You are dry
humping my
last nerve

You Are Dry Humping My Last Nerve

XXXXXXXXXXXXXXXXXXXXXXXXXXXXXX

Design by Cranky Cat Cross Stitch

When you need to let them know that life is too short for their crap.

COLOR CHART

COLOR BLOCK	FLOSS NUMBER	COLOR NAME	STITCHES	STRANDS	SKEINS
⊘	310	Black	885	2	1
✳	791	Very Dark Cornflower Blue	1532	2	1
♎	794	Light Cornflower Blue	882	2	1
C	3747	Very Light Blue Violet	496	2	1
⬮	3807	Cornflower Blue	890	2	1

PATTERN INFORMATION

FABRIC: 14-count Aida, 15 x 12 in (38 x 30.5 cm)

NEEDLE: Size 24 tapestry

STITCH COUNT: 129 x 82

FINISHED SIZE: 9.2 x 5.8 in (23.39 x 15.16 cm)

MOUNTING: Piece will fit into a 9 x 11 in picture frame

SIZE VARIATIONS

12-count Aida: 10.75 x 6.83 in (27.31 x 17.35 cm)

16-count Aida: 8.06 x 5.13 in (20.47 x 13.03 cm)

18-count Aida: 7.17 x 4.56 in (18.21 x 11.58 cm)

Project shown is stitched on 14-count, ivory Aida cloth and is mounted in a 10 x 12 in frame.

COLOR CHART

COLOR BLOCK	FLOSS NUMBER
⊘	310
✳	791
⚖	794
C	3747
◯	3807

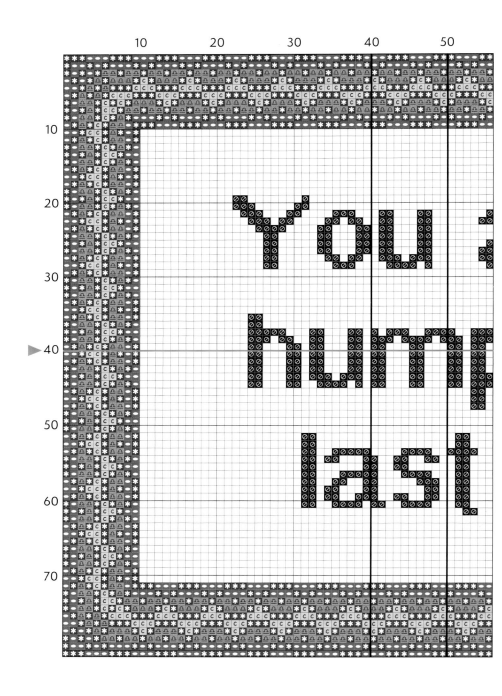

PLEASE GRANT ME THE SERENITY TO RESIST CUTTING A BITCH TODAY

Please Grant Me the Serenity to Resist Cutting a Bitch Today

X X X X X X X X X X X X X X X X X X X X X X X X X X X X X X X X X X X

Design by Jack the Stitcher

For those times you need a little divine intervention to save you from the hoosegow.

COLOR CHART

COLOR BLOCK	FLOSS NUMBER	COLOR NAME	STITCHES	STRANDS	SKEINS
■	310	Black	1393	2	2
	321	Christmas Red	54	2	1
	435	Brown Very light	180	2	1
	517	Wedgewood Dark	72	2	1
	519	Sky Blue	389	2	1
	742	Tangerine Light	69	2	1
M	743	Yellow medium	86	2	1
C	798	Delft Blue dark	693	2	1
	801	Coffee Brown dark	88	2	1
	898	Coffee Brown very dark	510	2	1
O	909	Emerald Green Very Dark	352	2	1
S	910	Emerald Green Dark	138	2	1
I	912	Emerald Green Light	368	2	1
✖	970	Pumpkin Light	72	2	1
	3760	Wedgewood (806)	158	2	1
	3799	Pewter Grey Very Dark	170	2	1
	3834	Grape Dark	216	2	1
	3835	Grape Medium	132	2	1
A	3836	Grape Light	48	2	1
✤	BLANC	White	92	2	1

PATTERN INFORMATION

FABRIC: 14-count Aida, 15 x 15 in (38 x 38 cm)

NEEDLE: Size 24 tapestry

STITCH COUNT: 123 x 123

FINISHED SIZE: 8.9 x 8.9 in (22.5 x 22.5 cm)

MOUNTING: Piece will fit into a 9 in or 10 in square picture frame (if you prefer a border)

SIZE VARIATIONS

12-count Aida: 11.67 x 8.33 in (29.64 x 21.16 cm)

16-count Aida: 8.75 x 6.25 in (22.23 x 15.88 cm)

18-count Aida: 7.78 x 5.56 in (19.76 x 14.12 cm)

Project shown is stitched on 14-count, ivory Aida cloth and mounted in a 10 in square frame.

COLOR CHART

COLOR BLOCK	FLOSS NUMBER
■	310
▨	321
✳	435
♉	517
⊡	519
☿	742
M	743
C	798
⠶	801
⠶	898
O	909
§	910
I	912
✖	970
♈	3760
↻	3799
●	3834
☾	3835
A	3836
♣	BLANC

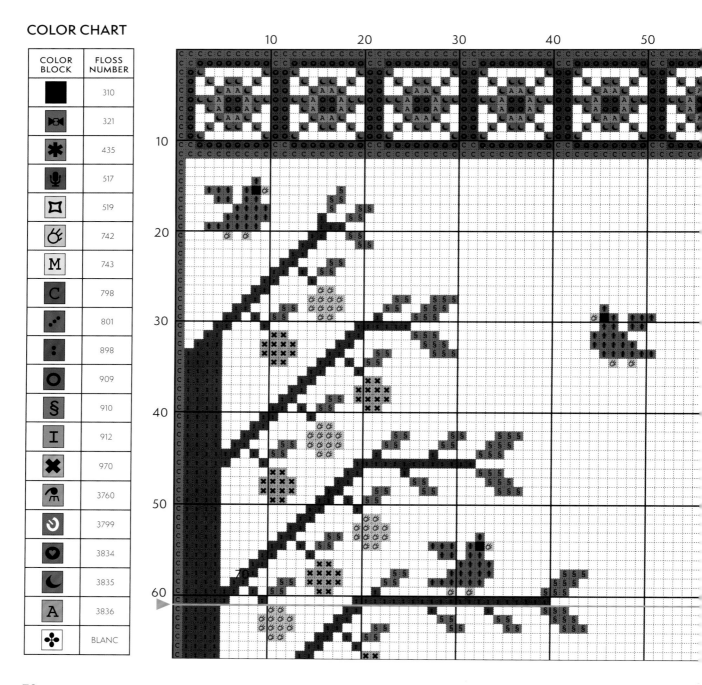

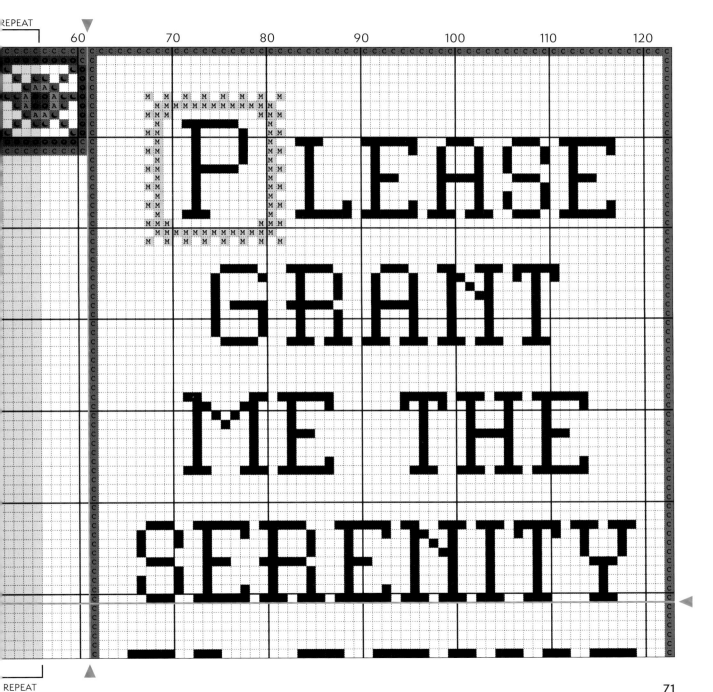

COLOR CHART

COLOR BLOCK	FLOSS NUMBER
■	310
▶◀	321
✳	435
♇	517
¤	519
♂	742
M	743
C	798
⋰	801
⋮	898
O	909
§	910
I	912
✖	970
⋒	3760
ᴐ	3799
●	3834
☾	3835
A	3836
♣	BLANC

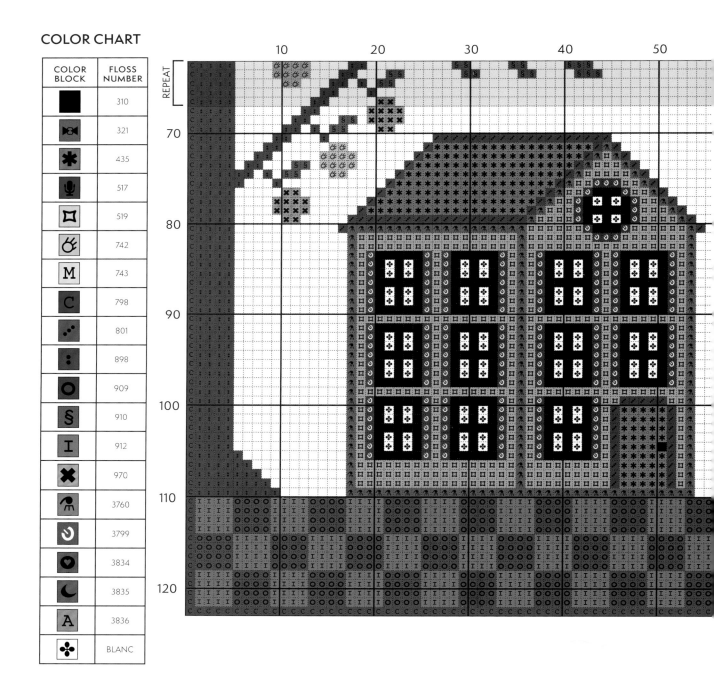

FUCKING YIKES

Design by Stephanie Rohr of stephXstitch

When you want to go retro with your expletives.

COLOR CHART

COLOR BLOCK	FLOSS NUMBER	COLOR NAME	STITCHES	STRANDS	SKEINS
▲	209	Dark Lavender	150	2	1
●	340	Medium Blue Violet	120	2	1
⬆	600	Very Dark Cranberry	159	2	1
◘	604	Light Cranberry	232	2	1
>	819	Light Baby Pink	153	2	1
↗	915	Dark Plum	153	2	1
✳	3753	Ultra Very Light Antique Blue	259	2	1
◆	3837	Ultra Dark Lavender	19	2	1

PATTERN INFORMATION

FABRIC: 14-count Aida, black, 10 x 9 in (25.4 x 22.9 cm)

NEEDLE: Size 24 tapestry

STITCH COUNT: 64 x 44

FINISHED SIZE: 4.6 x 3.1 in (11.6 x 7.8 cm)

MOUNTING: Piece will fit into a 4 x 6 in picture frame or 6 in embroidery hoop

SIZE VARIATIONS

12-count Aida: 5.3 x 3.7 in (13.46 x 9.4 cm)

16-count Aida: 4 x 2.75 in (10.16 x 6.99 cm)

18-count Aida: 3.5 x 2.4 in (8.89 x 6.1 cm)

Project shown is stitched on 14-count, black Aida cloth and mounted in a 6 in hoop.

A LITTLE FUCKING HELP, PLEASE!

For tips on working with black Aida cloth, see page 125.

COLOR CHART

COLOR BLOCK	FLOSS NUMBER
▲	209
●	340
⬆	600
▣	604
>	819
↗	915
✳	3753
◆	3837

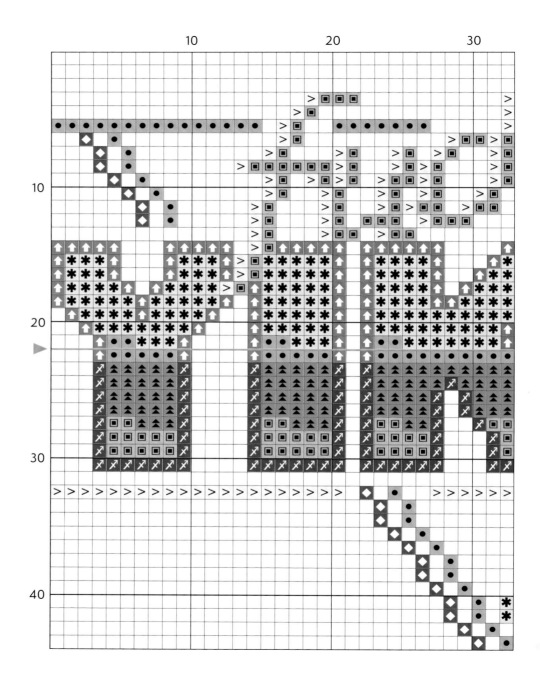

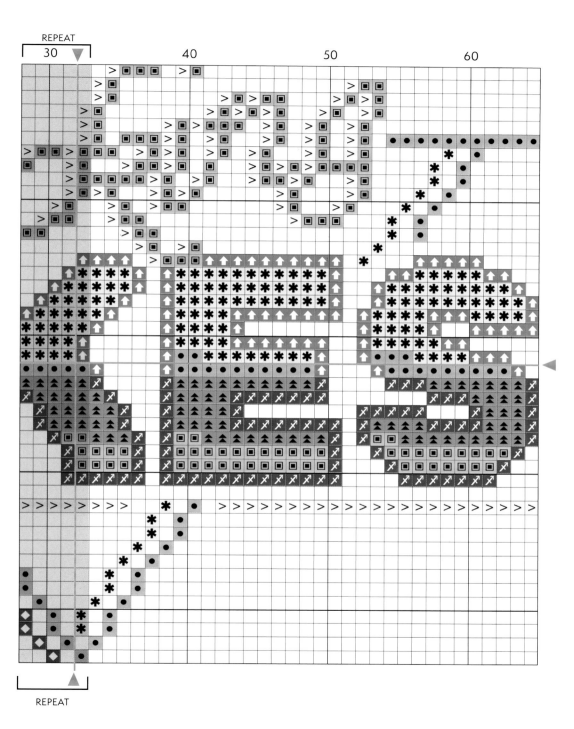

HOLY SHIT I LOVE YOU!

Design by EZBakedCrafts

When you want to send the very fucking best.

COLOR CHART

COLOR BLOCK	FLOSS NUMBER	COLOR NAME	STITCHES	STRANDS	SKEINS
⋮	608	Bright Orange	62	2	1
▶	892	Carnation	775	2	1
▼	906	Parrot Green	668	2	1
△	963	Dusty Rose	78	2	1
●	973	Bright Canary	40	2	1

PATTERN INFORMATION

FABRIC: 14-count Aida, 11 x 11 in (28 x 28 cm)

NEEDLE: Size 24 tapestry

STITCH COUNT: 70 x 70

FINISHED SIZE: 5 x 5 in (12.7 x 12.7 cm)

MOUNTING: Piece will fit into a 6 in round hoop

SIZE VARIATIONS

12-count Aida: 5.83 x 5.83 in (14.81 x 14.81 cm)

16-count Aida: 4.38 x 4.38 in (11.13 x 11.13 cm)

18-count Aida: 3.89 x 3.89 in (9.88 x 9.88 cm)

Project shown is stitched on 16-count, white Aida cloth and mounted in a 5 in hoop.

STITCHING NOTE

The flower stems and outlines of the text are done in backstitch with DMC floss 906. For instruction on this stitch, see page 14.

COLOR CHART

COLOR BLOCK	FLOSS NUMBER
⦂	608
▶	892
◀▶	906
△	963
●	973

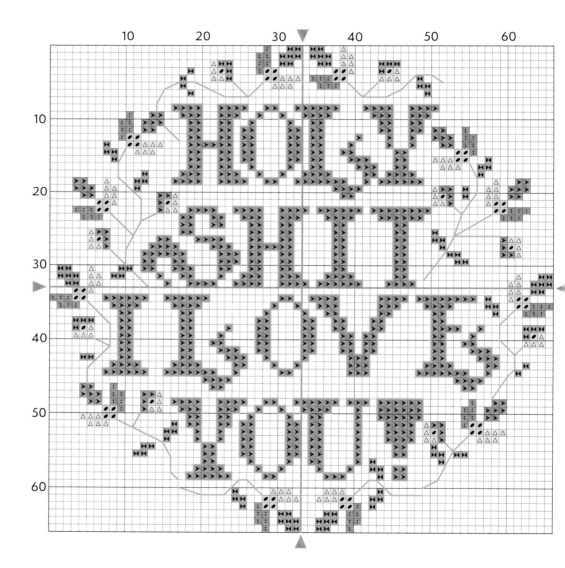

Stitch Your Own: Uppercase Alphabet

For the lowercase alphabet, see page 21.

Pew Pew Madafakas!

Design by Oh Wow Stitch

When threatening and hilariously cute collide.

COLOR CHART

COLOR BLOCK	FLOSS NUMBER	COLOR NAME	STITCHES	STRANDS	SKEINS
⌂	310	Black	2894	2	2
▲	606	Bright Orange-Red	559	2	1
◉	721	Medium Orange Spice	338	2	1
⌁	742	Light Tangerine	214	2	1
♥	815	Medium Garnet	239	2	1
★	3782	Light Mocha Brown	146	2	1
☾	3821	Straw	237	2	1
⚡	3847	Dark Teal Green	387	2	1
K	3848	Medium Teal Green	199	2	1
◯	B5200	Snow White	38	2	1

PATTERN INFORMATION

FABRIC: 16-count Aida, 12 x 12 in (30.5 x 30.5 cm)

NEEDLE: Size 24 tapestry

STITCH COUNT: 89 x 84

FINISHED SIZE: 5.6 x 5.2 in (16.25 x 13.5 cm)

MOUNTING: Piece will fit into an 8 in hoop

SIZE VARIATIONS

12-count Aida: 7.42 x 7 in (18.85 x 17.78 cm)

14-count Aida: 6.36 x 6 in (16.21 x 15.24 cm)

18-count Aida: 4.94 x 4.67 in (12.55 x 11.86 cm)

Project shown is stitched on 14-count, black Aida cloth and mounted in a 9 in hoop.

A LITTLE FUCKING HELP, PLEASE!

For tips on working with black Aida cloth, see page 125.

COLOR CHART

COLOR BLOCK	FLOSS NUMBER
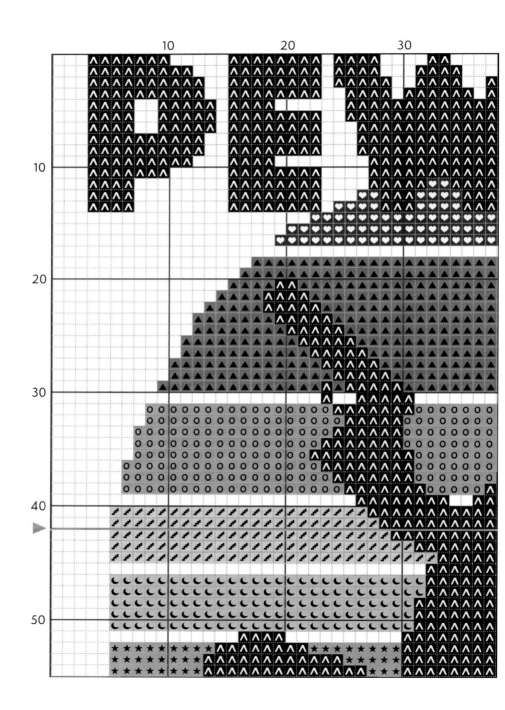	310
	606
	721
	742
	815
	3782
	3821
	3847
	3848
	B5200

84

COLOR CHART

COLOR BLOCK	FLOSS NUMBER
∧	310
▲	606
O	721
◢	742
♥	815
★	3782
☾	3821
⚡	3847
K	3848
O	B5200

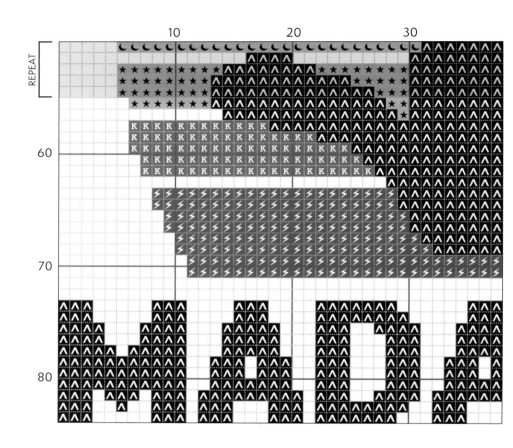

STITCHING NOTE

For a denser-looking stitch, Oh Wow Stitch suggests working the pattern on 16-count Aida; however, if you prefer a more "cross-stitch" look, where the Xs are more visible (as shown in the photo on page 82), use 14-count Aida.

VARIATION

For ease of use, the pattern is shown here with a white
background and black text; if you want to create the
project as shown in the picture on page 82, just use the
white (DMC B5200) floss instead of black for the text
and increase the number of white skeins to two. All of the
other colors stay the same.

Oh Hell No

Design by Grandma Girl Designs

Shut them down with a little skull and cross-stitch.

COLOR CHART

COLOR BLOCK	FLOSS NUMBER	COLOR NAME	STITCHES	STRANDS	SKEINS
■	310	Black	3806	2	2
■	666	Bright Red	1532	2	1

PATTERN INFORMATION

FABRIC: 14-count Aida, 15 x 15 in (38 x 38 cm)

NEEDLE: Size 24 tapestry

STITCH COUNT: 125 x 125

FINISHED SIZE: 8.9 x 8.9 in

MOUNTING: Piece will fit into a 10 in hoop

SIZE VARIATIONS

12-count Aida: 9.58 x 8 in (24.56 x 20.32 cm)

14-count Aida: 8.21 x 6.86 in (20.85 x 17.42 cm)

18-count Aida: 6.39 x 5.33 in (16.23 x 13.53 cm)

Project shown is stitched on 16-count, white Aida cloth and mounted in a 9-in hoop.

A LITTLE FUCKING HELP, PLEASE!

There is a lot of counting in this one, so here is a time-saving (and possibly headache-reducing) tip: Stitch the entire piece (or sections, if you like) in a single diagonal stitch (the first half of the cross-stitch); that way, if you miscount, you only have single stitches to rip out. Also, when you go back to fill in the other half of the stitches, you won't have to be tied to the book—the pattern is right in front of you!

For a denser look, Grandma Girl suggests doing this project on 18-count Aida, using a size 28 tapestry needle.

COLOR BLOCK	FLOSS NUMBER
■	310
■	666

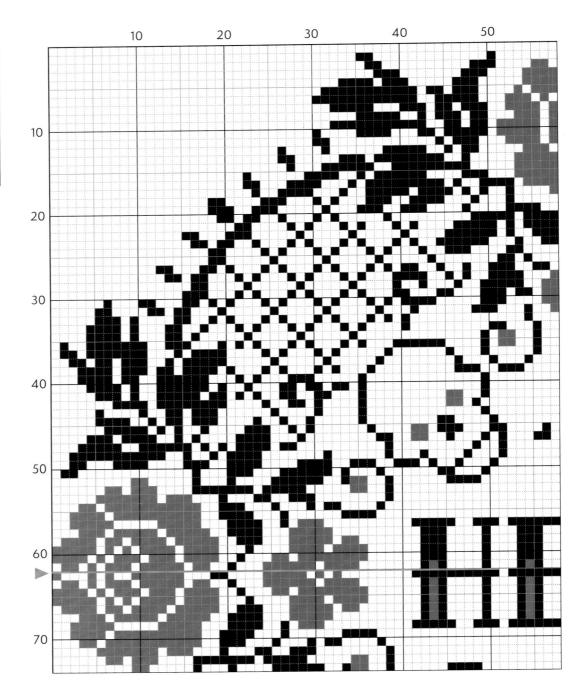

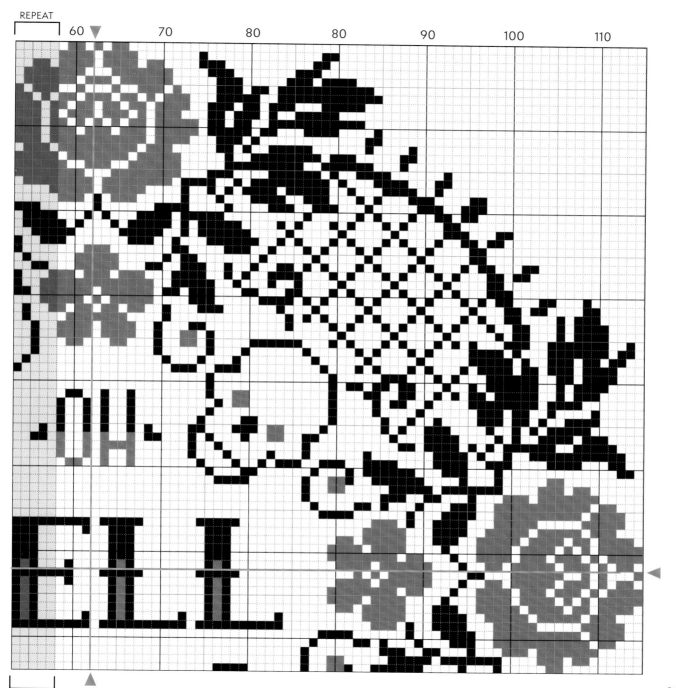

COLOR CHART

COLOR BLOCK	FLOSS NUMBER
■	310
■	666

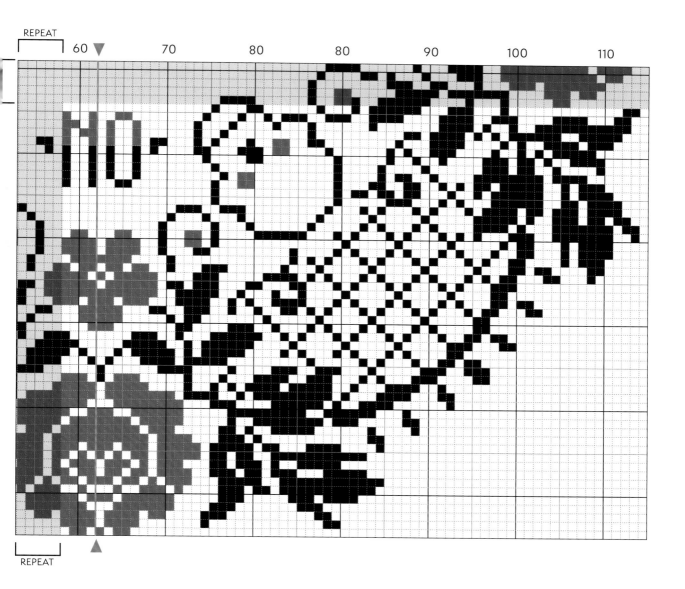

WELCOME TO THE SHITSHOW

Design by BeCoProductions

Telling it like it is.

COLOR CHART

COLOR BLOCK	FLOSS NUMBER	COLOR NAME	STITCHES	STRANDS	SKEINS
▲	310	Black	60 (+325 outline)	3	1
⊠	699	Green	55	3	1
✕	703	Chartreuse	46	3	1
⬤	760	Salmon	166	3	1
◆	818	Baby Pink	128	3	1
▤	893	Light Carnation	182	3	1
✿	3689	Light Mauve	133	3	1

PATTERN INFORMATION

FABRIC: 14-count Aida, 11 x 10 in (28 x 25.4 cm)

NEEDLE: Size 24 tapestry

STITCH COUNT: 63 x 55

FINISHED SIZE: 4.5 x 3.9 in

MOUNTING: Piece will fit into a 6 in hoop

SIZE VARIATIONS

12-count Aida: 5.25 x 4.58 in (13.34 x 11.63 cm)

14-count Aida: 4.5 x 3.93 in (11.43 x 9.98 cm)

18-count Aida: 3.5 x 3.06 in (8.98 x 7.77 cm)

Project shown is stitched on 14-count, white Aida cloth and mounted in a 6 in hoop.

STITCHING NOTE

The straight lines in this project are not backstitch, but straight stitch. This stitch uses a similar technique to backstitch, but just goes over a longer area. You come up at the beginning of the line, and back down into the canvas at the end of the line, pulling the thread taut so it lies flat on the canvas. Follow the pattern to determine the length of every straight stitch.

COLOR CHART

COLOR BLOCK	FLOSS NUMBER
▲	310
⊠	699
✕	703
⬤	760
◢	818
▤	893
✷	3689

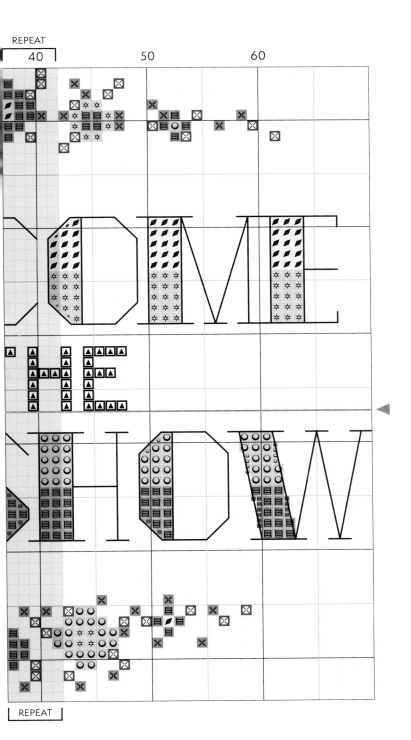

Behold! The Field in Which I Grow My Fucks/ Lay Thine Eyes Upon It and See That It Is Barren

XXXXXXXXXXXXXXXXXXXXXXXXXXXXXXXXXX

Design by EZBakedCrafts

When you want to sound ultra-literate with your kiss-off.

COLOR CHART

COLOR BLOCK	FLOSS NUMBER	COLOR NAME	STITCHES	STRANDS	SKEINS
⠿	09	Very Dark Cocoa		2	2
◗	680	Dark Old Gold		2	1
2	842	Very Light Beige Brown		2	1
↙	890	Ultra Dark Pistachio Green		2	1
O	956	Geranium		2	1
//	972	Dark Canary		2	1
◆	Diamant 3821	Straw		3	1*

PATTERN INFORMATION

FABRIC: 14-count Aida, 15 x 15 in (38 x 38 cm)

NEEDLE: Size 24 tapestry

STITCH COUNT: 126 x 126

FINISHED SIZE: 9 x 9 in (22.9 x 22.9 cm)

MOUNTING: Piece will fit into a 10 in round hoop

SIZE VARIATIONS

12-count Aida: 10.5 x 10.5 in (26.67 x 26.67 cm)

16-count Aida: 7.88 x 7.88 in (20.02 x 20.02 cm)

18-count Aida: 7 x 7 in (17.78 x 17.78 cm)

Project shown is stitched on 14-count, ivory Aida cloth and mounted in a 10 in hoop.

*NOTE: The Diamant thread comes in a spool instead of a skein, and only has three strands instead of six, like the floss. Use all three strands.

COLOR CHART

COLOR BLOCK	FLOSS NUMBER
⦂	09
◗	680
2	842
↙	890
O	956
//	972
✦	Diamant 3821

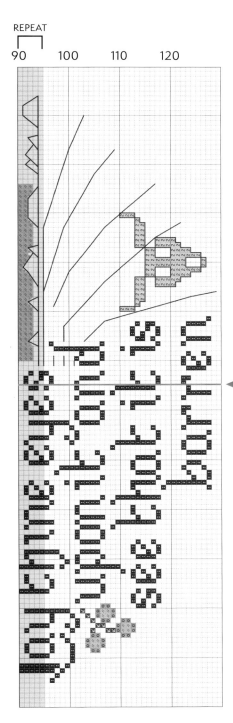

A LITTLE FUCKING HELP, PLEASE!

- Gold metallic thread can sometimes be a real bitch to use. If you want to make things easier on yourself, you can use two strands of Old Gold floss (676) instead.

- The outline of the cow skull and the lines of the barren desert are done in backstitch, using DMC 09 floss. For instruction on how to do backstitch, see page 14.

I Am
A
Delicate
Fucking
Flower

I Am a Delicate Fucking Flower

XXXXXXXXXXXXXXXXXXXXXXXXXXXXXXXXXXXXXX

Design by Snarky Stitch Bitch

When people need to be reminded what a damned refined person you are.

COLOR CHART

COLOR BLOCK	FLOSS NUMBER	COLOR NAME	STITCHES	STRANDS	SKEINS
//	307	Lemon	453	2	1
▲▼	310	Black	1255	2	1
◈	444	Lemon Dark	94	2	1
◤	904	Parrot Green Very Dark	126	2	1
○	905	Parrot Green Dark	185	2	1
器	973	Canary Bright	104	2	1

PATTERN INFORMATION

FABRIC: 14-count Aida, 12 x 13 in (30.5 x 33 cm)

NEEDLE: Size 24 tapestry

STITCH COUNT: 82 x 94

FINISHED SIZE: 5.9 x 6.8 in (15 x 17.3 cm)

MOUNTING: Piece will fit into a 10 in embroidery hoop or an 8 x 10 in picture frame

SIZE VARIATIONS

12-count Aida: 6.83 x 7.83 in (17.35 x 19.89 cm)

16-count Aida: 5.13 x 5.88 in (13.03 x 14.94 cm)

18-count Aida: 4.56 x 5.22 in (11.58 x 13.26 cm)

Project shown is stitched on 14-count, white Aida and mounted in a 10 in frame.

COLOR CHART

COLOR BLOCK	FLOSS NUMBER
//	307
◩	310
◈	444
◩	904
◉	905
✿	973

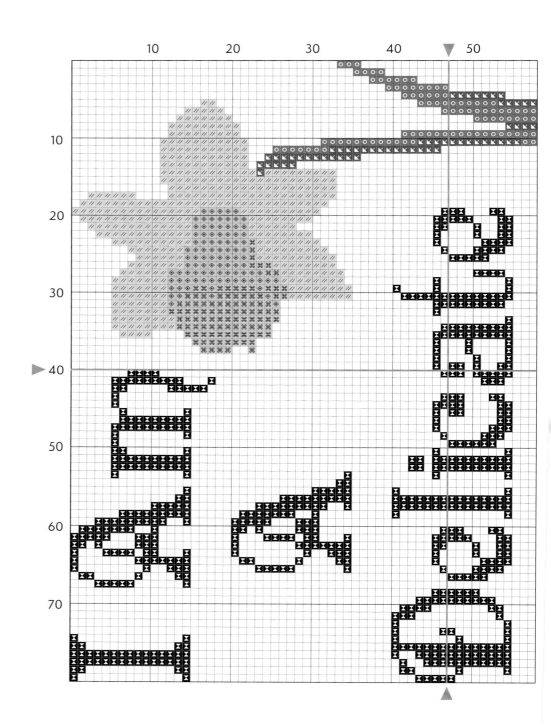

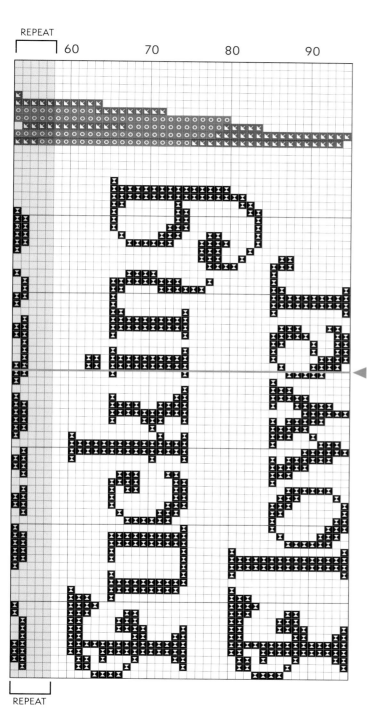

60 70 80 90

BITCH.
PLEASE.

Bitch, Please.

Design by Cranky Cat Cross Stitch

When eye-rolling doesn't cut it.

COLOR CHART

COLOR BLOCK	FLOSS NUMBER	COLOR NAME	STITCHES	STRANDS	SKEINS
⊘	158	Medium Very Dark Cornflower Blue	370	2	1
⦂	310	Black	1582	2	1
◖	500	Very Dark Blue Green	398	2	1
✖	501	Dark Blue Green	368	2	1
♠	502	Blue Green	594	2	1
●	503	Medium Blue Green	610	2	1
⊃	504	Very Light Blue Green	132	2	1
O	554	Light Violet	521	2	1
Ω	794	Light Cornflower Blue	646	2	1
⬆	3807	Cornflower Blue	629	2	1

PATTERN INFORMATION

FABRIC: 14-count Aida, 12 x 13 in (30.5 x 33 cm)

NEEDLE: Size 24 tapestry

STITCH COUNT: 82 x 94

FINISHED SIZE: 5.9 x 6.8 in (15 x 17.3 cm)

MOUNTING: Piece will fit into an 10 in embroidery hoop or an 8 x 10 in picture frame

SIZE VARIATIONS

12-count Aida: 6.83 x 7.83 in (17.35 x 19.89 cm)

16-count Aida: 5.13 x 5.88 in (13.03 x 14.94 cm)

18-count Aida: 4.56 x 5.22 in (11.58 x 13.26 cm)

Project shown is stitched on 14-count, ivory Aida cloth and mounted in a 10 in frame.

COLOR CHART

COLOR BLOCK	FLOSS NUMBER
⬭	158
⬛	310
◗	500
✖	501
⬥	502
●	503
⟩	504
O	554
♎	794
⬆	3807

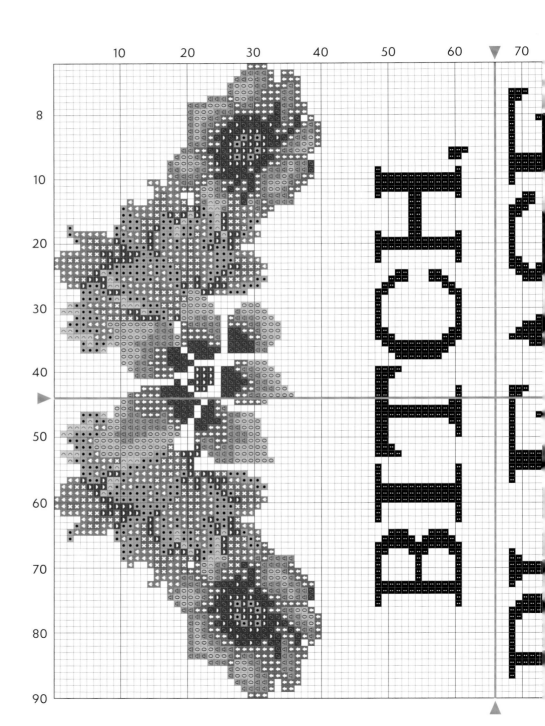

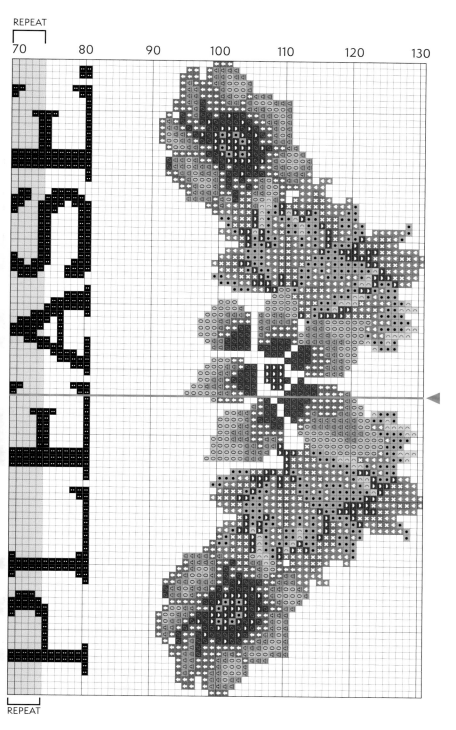

Fuck It

Design by Happy Sloth

Sometimes, there are just no two better words.

COLOR CHART

COLOR BLOCK	FLOSS NUMBER	COLOR NAME	STITCHES	STRANDS	SKEINS
⬛	310	Black	2158	2	2
⬜	335	Rose	980	2	1
⬜	368	Light Pistachio Green	431	2	1
⬜	597	Turquoise	780	2	1
⬜	598	Light Turquoise	656	2	1
⬜	676	Light Old Gold	28	2	1
⬜	727	Very Light Topaz	916	2	1
⬜	3831	Dark Raspberry	1001	2	1

PATTERN INFORMATION

FABRIC: 14-count Aida, 14 x 16 in (35.6 x 40.6 cm)

NEEDLE: Size 24 tapestry

STITCH COUNT: 110 x 120

FINISHED SIZE: 7.8 x 8.5 in (20 x 23.6 cm)

MOUNTING: Piece will fit into a 10 in hoop, or a 10 in square picture frame

SIZE VARIATIONS

12-count Aida: 11.67 x 8.33 in (29.64 x 21.16 cm)

16-count Aida: 8.75 x 6.25 in (22.23 x 15.88 cm)

18-count Aida: 7.78 x 5.56 in (19.76 x 14.12 cm)

Project shown is stitched on 14-count, white Aida cloth and mounted in a 10 in hoop.

COLOR CHART

COLOR BLOCK	FLOSS NUMBER
⬛	310
⬛	335
⬛	368
⬛	597
⬛	598
⬛	676
⬜	727
⬛	3831

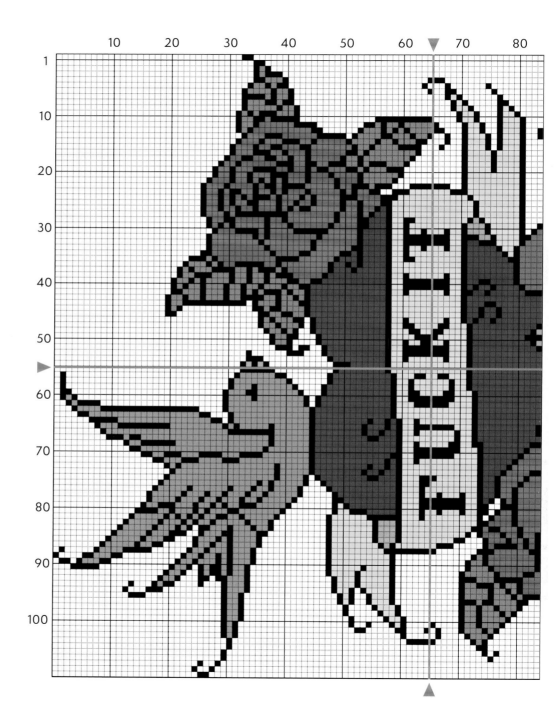

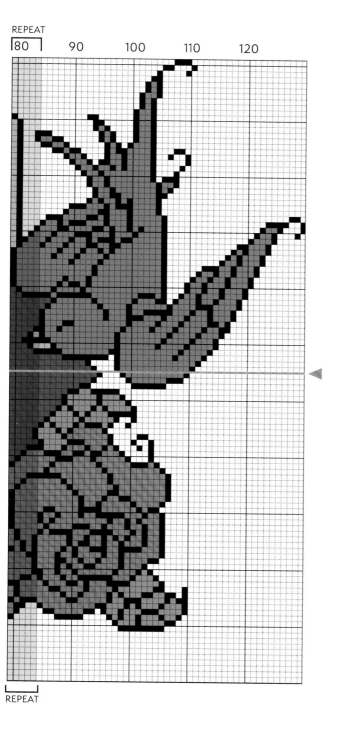

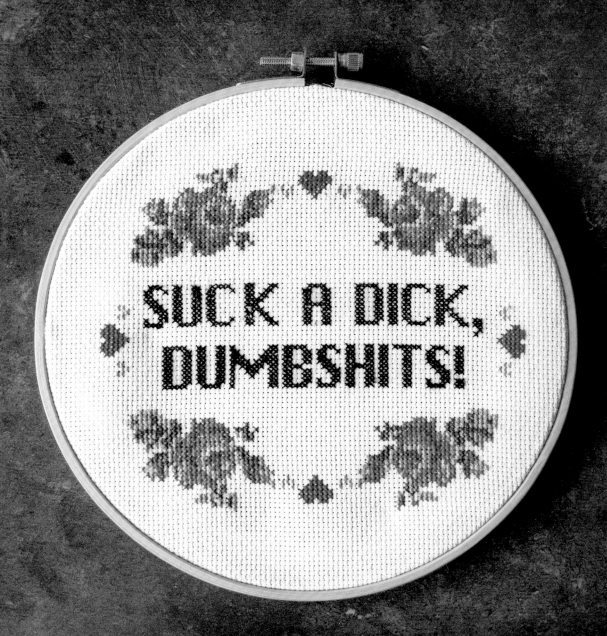

SUCK A DICK, DUMBSHITS!

Design by Grandma Girl Designs

When you just need to just shut. it. down.

COLOR CHART

COLOR BLOCK	FLOSS NUMBER	COLOR NAME	STITCHES	STRANDS	SKEINS
◻	310	Black	586	3	1
◪	561	Very Dark Jade	228	3	1
✚	563	Light Jade	292	3	1
▽	600	Very Dark Cranberry	244	3	1
◖	602	Medium Cranberry	320	3	1
⊘	603	Cranberry	172	3	1
♡	605	Very Light Cranberry	224	3	1

PATTERN INFORMATION

FABRIC: 14-count Aida, 13 x 12 in (33 x 30.5 cm)

NEEDLE: Size 24 tapestry

STITCH COUNT: 89 x 74

FINISHED SIZE: 6.4 x 5.3 in (16.25 x 13.5 cm)

MOUNTING: Piece will fit into an 8 in hoop

SIZE VARIATIONS

12-count Aida: 7.42 x 6.17 in (18.85 x 15.67 cm)

16-count Aida: 5.56 x 4.63 in (14.12 x 11.76 cm)

18-count Aida: 4.94 x 4.11 in (12.55 x 10.44 cm)

Project shown is stitched in 14-count, white Aida cloth and mounted in an 8 in hoop.

STITCHING NOTE

Grandma Girl Designs prefers using three strands of floss for a denser appearance to the stitches; but if you prefer a more "cross-stitch" look, where the Xs are more visible, you can work the pattern with just two strands.

COLOR CHART

COLOR BLOCK	FLOSS NUMBER
⬜	310
◼	561
✛	563
▽	600
◖	602
⊘	603
♡	605

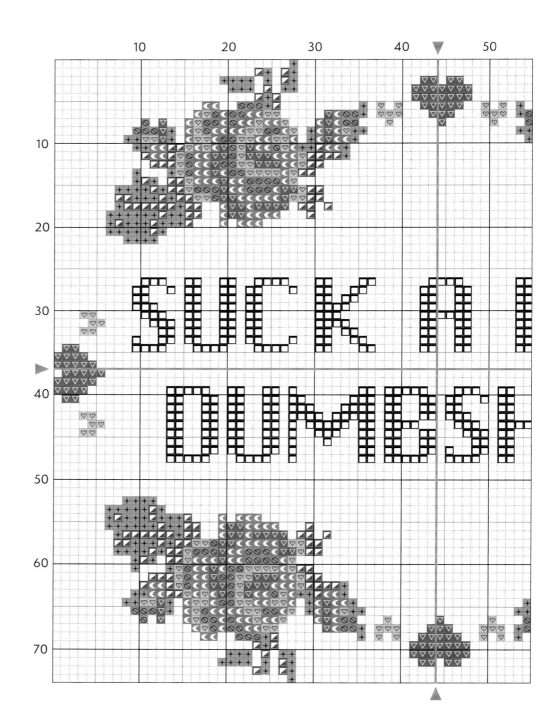

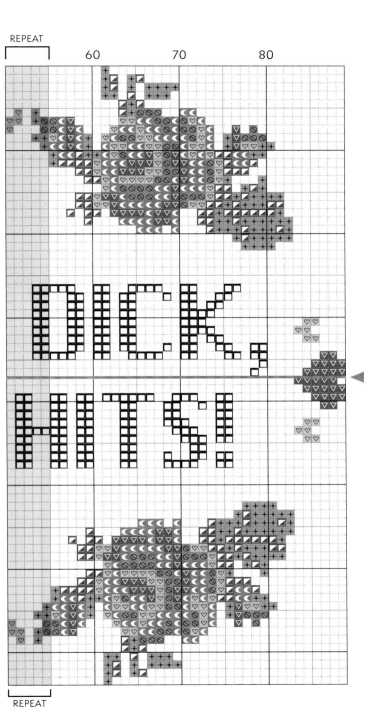

THE SHORT ANSWER IS

NO

THE LONG ANSWER IS

FUCK NO

THE SHORT ANSWER IS NO / THE LONG ANSWER IS FUCK NO

XXXXXXXXXXXXXXXXXXXXXXXXXXXXXXXXXX

Design by Cranky Cat Cross Stitch

Some people always need the damned long answer.

COLOR CHART

COLOR BLOCK	FLOSS NUMBER	COLOR NAME	STITCHES	STRANDS	SKEINS
■	310	Black	4171	2	2
♠	312	Very Dark Baby Blue	724	2	1
⬚	3755	Baby Blue	660	2	1
⊠	3841	Pale Baby Blue	338	2	1

PATTERN INFORMATION

FABRIC: 14-count Aida, 16 x 13 in (40.6 x 33 cm)

NEEDLE: Size 24 tapestry

STITCH COUNT: 140 x 100

FINISHED SIZE: 10 x 7.14 in (25.4 x 18.14 cm)

MOUNTING: Piece will fit into an 11 x 14 in picture frame

SIZE VARIATIONS

12-count Aida: 11.67 x 8.33 in (29.64 x 21.16 cm)

16-count Aida: 8.75 x 6.25 in (22.23 x 15.88 cm)

18-count Aida: 7.78 x 5.56 in (19.76 x 14.12 cm)

Project shown is stitched on 14-count, white Aida and mounted in a 9 x 11 in frame.

COLOR CHART

COLOR BLOCK	FLOSS NUMBER
■	310
♠	312
⠢	3755
⋈	3841

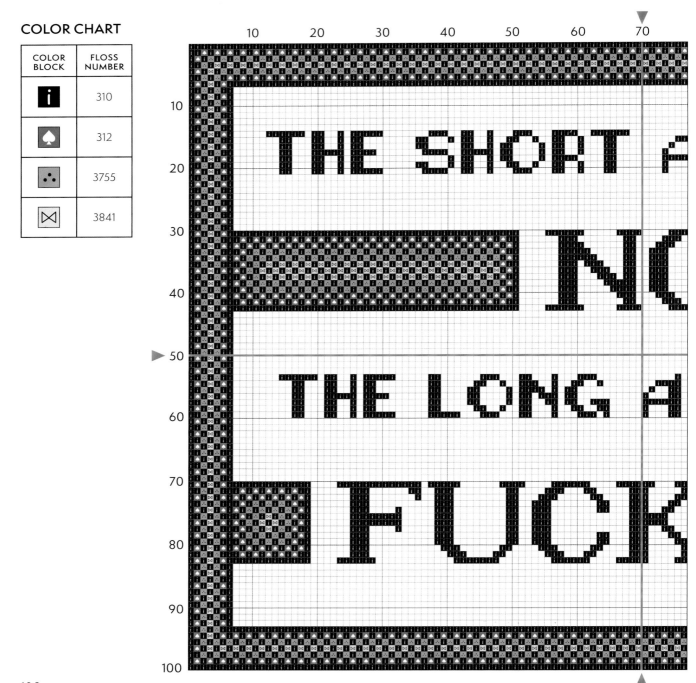

WELL, SHIT.

Design by Aliton Embroidery

Sometimes, that's all there is to say.

COLOR CHART

COLOR BLOCK	FLOSS NUMBER	COLOR NAME	STITCHES	STRANDS	SKEINS
x	349	Dark Coral	194	2	1
T	741	Medium Tangerine	360	2	1
o	743	Medium Yellow	510	2	1
e	817	Very Dark Coral Red	384	2	1
n	905	Dark Parrot Green	269	2	1
L	907	Light Parrot Green	158	2	1
H	3705	Dark Melon	682	2	1
a	3801	Very Dark Melon	184	2	1
Y	3837	Ultra Dark Lavender	274	2	1

PATTERN INFORMATION

FABRIC: 14-count Aida, 12 x 12 in (30. 5 x 30.5 cm)

NEEDLE: Size 24 tapestry

STITCH COUNT: 84 x 84

FINISHED SIZE: 6 x 6 in (15.2 x 15.2 cm)

MOUNTING: Piece will fit into a 7 or 8 in hoop

SIZE VARIATIONS

12-count Aida: 7 x 7 in (17.78 x 17.78 cm)

14-count Aida: 6 x 6 in (15.24 x 15.24 cm)

18-count Aida: 4.67 x 4.67 in (11.86 x 11.86 cm)

Project shown is stitched in 14-count, ivory Aida cloth and mounted in a 7 in frame.

COLOR CHART

COLOR BLOCK	FLOSS NUMBER
X	349
T	741
o	743
e	817
n	905
L	907
H	3705
a	3801
Y	3837

A LITTLE FUCKING HELP, PLEASE!

This project also looks fantastic stitched on black Aida. Black Aida cloth can sometimes be tricky to use, as the holes are harder to see. To help make them more visible, place a light-colored towel or piece of paper under the hoop (on your lap is easiest).

MEET THE ARTISTS

And now, a word about our artists—from the artists!

8 Bit Stitch

I'll Be Damned., page 56

8 Bit Stitch was established in 2013 by Kari Warning. It started as an Etsy shop filled with finished cross-stitch and crochet items. It has since transformed into a hub for cross-stitch patterns. The pattern featured in this book is a tribute to a phrase used often by her grandfather. For more of Kari's work, visit www.8bitstitch.com or www.etsy.com/shop/8bitstitching, or follow Kari on Instagram @8.bit.stitch and YouTube at www.Youtube.com/c/8bitstitch.

Aliton Embroidery

I Wish I Was a Unicorn So I Could Stab Stupid People with My Head, page 26
Well, Shit., page 122

The Aliton Embroidery team has been working since 2017. You can see more of their work at alitonembroidery.net and follow them on Instagram, Facebook, Pinterest, and Twitter at @alitonembroidery.

BeCoProductions

Welcome to the Shitshow, page 94

Andrea is the creator behind BeCoProductions; an embroidery/cross-stitch shop that offers custom pieces, ready-made finished hoops, and, of course, embroidery and cross-stitch patterns. Andrea has been embroidering since 2015, but has only recently started making patterns last year; there is a mix of beginner and advanced projects, and of course the occasional sassy stitch, like this cross-stitch here. Visit our Etsy store at www.becoproductions.etsy.com, and follow us on Instagram at @becoproductions.

TheChillNeedle

No Shit, page 22
Shut Up, page 50

Hi, there ! I'm Simon, a Frenchy cross-stitch pattern maker. For me, cross-stitching is a peaceful moment, out of time, you take for yourself to create and focus. If for you meditation is boring, you should try cross-stitch! Take a deep breath and relax, it's Cross-stitch Time! Wanna see more? Check my store on Etsy: https://www.etsy.com/shop/thechillneedle, or my Instagram @thechillneedle.

Cranky Cat Cross Stitch

You are Dry Humping My Last Nerve, page 64
Bitch, Please., page 106
The Short Answer is No / The Long Answer is Fuck No, page 118

K. E. Hann started designing cross-stitch as a method of PTSD therapy, soon branching out from geometrics into florals and more, most designs bearing her signature snark. Hann also uses her designs to promote and fundraise for humanitarian causes, including the lost residential schoolchildren in Canada, refugee support, and war relief. Find more of her designs at Etsy: www.etsy.com/ca/shop/CrankyCatCrossStitch.

EZBakedCrafts

Holy Shit I Love You!, page 78
Behold! The Field in Which I Grow My Fucks / Lay Thine Eyes Upon it and See That It Is Barren, page 98

Aimee Savey was an avid knitter before the pandemic, but after knitting nine sweaters back-to-back during quarantine, she turned to snarky cross-stitching to occupy that nervous energy at a fraction of the cost. She also like tattoos and cats. Her patterns can be found at @EZBakedCrafts on Etsy.

Grandma Girl Designs

Oh HELL No, page 88

Suck a Dick, Dumbshits!, page 114

Grandma Girl Designs is run by Los Angeles native Erica Estrada. Her cross-stitch patterns and products are inspired by dark humor, nostalgia, and random fandom. She highly recommends stitching to the soothing sounds of angry TV housewives. Find her patterns, kits, and stitching accessories at grandmagirldesigns.com or follow her on Instagram @grandmagirldesigns.

Happy Sloth

What the Actual Fuck, page 60

Fuck It, page 110

Happy Sloth Patterns is an indie cross-stitch brand run by Cherie and Circe. We're based in the colorful, creative hub of Melbourne, Australia. The brand specializes in irreverent feminist designs, with a good dose of snark. Visit us at HappySlothPatterns.com

Jack the Stitcher

Please Grant Me the Serenity to Resist Cutting a Bitch Today, page 68

Born and raised in New York, I grew up tearing through classic video games with my fellow clan of devoted nerds (a.k.a. my loving family). My Etsy shop displays a variation of patterns reflecting my unique sense of humor, but is mainly a collection of work built from self-care and warm childhood memories that I shared with my family. Visit my Etsy shop at: www.jackthestitcher.etsy.com

Oh Wow Stitch

Because Fuck You That's Why., page 34

Pew Pew Madafakas!, page 82

Katerina Youniacutt is the owner of OhWowStitch, based in Los Angeles, CA. She creates funny and sassy cross-stitch designs and sells them around the world. Visit her Etsy store at www.etsy.com/shop/OhWowStitch and follow her on Instagram at @oh_wow_stitch.

Snarky Stitch Bitch

The High Road Sucks as I'm Petty and Vindictive by Nature, page 44

I am a Delicate Fucking Flower, page 102

The Snarky Stitch Bitch creates subversive, feminist, media-centric cross-stitch patterns as part of her effort to overthrow the patriarchy. Her alter ego, Rebecca Owen, is a mild-mannered librarian who loves cats, cheese fries, and rewatching her favorite movies. Find more of her patterns on her website, Snarkystitchbitch.com, and on Etsy at SnarkyStitchBitch. You can also follow her on Instagram @snarkystitchbitch.

Stephanie Rohr of stephXstitch

Bollocks, page 18

Fucking Yikes, page 74

Stephanie Rohr is a Chicago-based cross-stitch designer who established her brand stephXstitch in 2010. She is the author of two pattern books: *Feminist Cross-Stitch* and *Self-Care Cross-Stitch*. You can find more of her work at stephXstitch.com and on Instagram, Facebook, Twitter, TikTok, Patreon, and Etsy @stephxstitch.

Stitchy Little Fox

Wash Your Damn Hands, page 30

Namaste Bitches, page 40

Cross-stitch started as a way to keep me entertained when my children were little and my husband was busy with his military duties, but it opened the door to a whole new world with amazing communities and fantastic people. My goal with StitchyLittleFox has always been to make people laugh. I create patterns that I think are funny, put them out in the world, and hope that someone else does, too. To see more of my designs, visit StitchyLittleFox.com, or follow me on Facebook at facebook.com/stitchylittlefox or Instagram at @stitchylittlefox.

weldon**owen**

an imprint of Insight Editions
P. O. Box 3088
San Rafael, CA 94912
www.weldonowen.com

CEO Raoul Goff
VP Publisher Roger Shaw
Editorial Director Katie Killebrew
Senior Editor Karyn Gerhard
VP Creative Chrissy Kwasnik
Senior Graphic Designer Judy Wiatrek Trum
VP Manufacturing Alix Nicholaeff
Senior Production Manager Joshua Smith
Senior Production Manager, Subsidiary Rights Lina s Palma-Temena

Text © 2023 Weldon Owen

Photographs of finished pieces by Jill Paice

Technical illustrations by Adam Raiti

Photo credits: **p.8, left**: Sue Chillingworth/Alamy Stock Photo; **p.8 right**: Katerina Minaeva/
Alamy Stock Photo; **p.9 top**: Aliaksandr Baiduk/Alamy Stock Photo; **p.9 bottom**: Sergei Finko/
Alamy Stock Photo.

Weldon Owen would like to thank the brilliant fucking people who helped put this book together:
proofreader Margaret Parrish, cross-stitcher Stacia Woodcock, editorial assistant Jon Ellis, and
photographer Jill Paice. A very special and heartfelt thanks to all of the fantastically talented
cross-stitch artists in this book, whose contributions have made this book so damned beautiful.

ISBN: 978-1-6818-8935-1

Printed in China by Insight Editions
First printed in 2023
10 9 8 7 6 5 4 3 2 1
2026 2025 2024 2023

ROOTS of PEACE   REPLANTED PAPER

Insight Editions, in association with Roots of Peace, will plant two trees for each tree used in the
manufacturing of this book. Roots of Peace is an internationally renowned humanitarian organization
dedicated to eradicating land mines worldwide and converting war-torn lands into productive farms
and wildlife habitats. Roots of Peace will plant two million fruit and nut trees in Afghanistan and
provide farmers there with the skills and support necessary for sustainable land use.